BALTIMORE CATECHISM TWO

Also known as

A CATECHISM *of* CHRISTIAN DOCTRINE NO. 2

Imprimatur: ✠ John Cardinal McCloskey
Archbishop of New York
New York, April 6, 1885

"The Catechism ordered by The Third Plenary Council of Baltimore, having been diligently compiled and examined, is hereby approved."

✠ James Gibbons
Archbishop of Baltimore
Apostolic Delegate
Baltimore, April 6, 1885

Imprimatur for Word Meanings:

Nihil obstat: ✠ Remy Lafort
Censor Librorum
New York, July 25, 1898

Imprimatur: ✠ Michael Augustine
Archbishop of New York
New York, July 25, 1898

Nihil obstat: ✠ Arthur J. Scanlan, S.T.D.
Censor Librorum
New York, November 26, 1932

Imprimatur: Patrick Cardinal Hayes
Archbishop of New York
New York, November 26, 1932

BALTIMORE CATECHISM TWO

Prepared and Enjoined by Order of
The Third Plenary Council of Baltimore

WITH PHONETICIZED WORDS, AND WORD MEANINGS

QUESTIONS NUMBERED TO AGREE WITH "EXPLANATION OF THE BALTIMORE CATECHISM"

With Prayers and Hymns

TAN·CLASSICS

TAN Books, a division of Saint Benedict Press, LLC.

Originally issued by the Third Plenary Council of Baltimore in 1885. This edition reprinted from the 1933 edition of Benziger Brothers, Inc. by arrangement with Benziger, Bruce and Glencoe, Inc.

Published with the assistance of The Livingstone Corporation. Cover and interior design by Mark Wainright, The Livingstone Corporation. Typeset by TAN Books.

Cover Image: *Christ among the doctors* by English School (20th century) Private Collection/Look and Learn/The Bridgeman Art Library.

ISBN: 978-0-89555-145-0

Printed and bound in India

13 12 11 10 9 8 7 6 5 4

www.TANBooks.com

CONTENTS

PRAYERS 1

CATECHISM

LESSON FIRST 7
On the End of Man

LESSON SECOND 11
On God and His Perfections

LESSON THIRD 13
On the Unity and Trinity of God

LESSON FOURTH 15
On Creation

LESSON FIFTH 17
On Our First Parents and the Fall

LESSON SIXTH 21
On Sin and Its Kinds

LESSON SEVENTH 23
On the Incarnation and Redemption

LESSON EIGHTH 27
On Our Lord's Passion, Death, Resurrection, and Ascension

LESSON NINTH 31
On the Holy Ghost and His Descent Upon the Apostles

LESSON TENTH 33
On the Effects of the Redemption

LESSON ELEVENTH 35
On the Church

LESSON TWELFTH 37
On the Attributes and Marks of the Church

LESSON THIRTEENTH 41
On the Sacraments in General

LESSON FOURTEENTH 45
On Baptism

LESSON FIFTEENTH 49
On Confirmation

LESSON SIXTEENTH 51
On the Gifts and Fruits of the Holy Ghost

LESSON SEVENTEENTH 55
On the Sacrament of Penance

LESSON EIGHTEENTH 59
On Contrition

LESSON NINETEENTH 63
On Confession

LESSON TWENTIETH 67
On the Manner of Making a Good Confession

LESSON TWENTY-FIRST 69
On Indulgences

LESSON TWENTY-SECOND 71
On the Holy Eucharist

LESSON TWENTY-THIRD 75
On the Ends for Which the Holy Eucharist Was Instituted

LESSON TWENTY-FOURTH 79
On the Sacrifice of the Mass

LESSON TWENTY-FIFTH 81
On Extreme Unction and Holy Orders

LESSON TWENTY-SIXTH 85
On Matrimony

LESSON TWENTY-SEVENTH 89
On the Sacramentals

LESSON TWENTY-EIGHTH 93
On Prayer

LESSON TWENTY-NINTH 95
On the Commandments of God

LESSON THIRTIETH 97
On the First Commandment

LESSON THIRTY-FIRST 101
The First Commandment—On the Honor and Invocation of the Saints

LESSON THIRTY-SECOND 105
From the Second to the Fourth Commandment

LESSON THIRTY-THIRD 109
From the Fourth to the Seventh Commandment

LESSON THIRTY-FOURTH 111
From the Seventh to the End of the Tenth Commandment

LESSON THIRTY-FIFTH 115
On the First and Second Commandments of the Church

LESSON THIRTY-SIXTH 119
On the Third, Fourth, Fifth, and Sixth Commandments of the Church

LESSON THIRTY-SEVENTH 123
On the Last Judgment and the Resurrection, Hell, Purgatory, and Heaven

MORNING PRAYERS 127

EVENING PRAYERS 129

PRAYERS FOR MASS 131

THE RIGHT MANNER OF CONFESSING 141

COMMUNION PRAYERS 143

THE ROSARY OF THE BLESSED VIRGIN 147

THE STATIONS OF THE CROSS 149

HYMNS 151

PRAYERS

The Lord's Prayer

Our Father, Who art in Heaven, hallowed be Thy name; Thy kingdom come; Thy will be done on earth as it is in Heaven. Give us this day our daily bread; and forgive us our trespasses as we forgive those who trespass against us: and lead us not into temptation, but deliver us from evil. Amen.

The Angelical Salutation

Hail Mary, full of grace! The Lord is with thee: blessed art thou amongst women, and blessed is the fruit of thy womb, Jesus. Holy Mary, Mother of God, pray for us sinners, now and at the hour of our death. Amen.

The Apostles' Creed

I believe in God, the Father Almighty, Creator of Heaven and earth; and in Jesus Christ, His only Son, Our Lord; who was conceived by the Holy Ghost, born of the Virgin Mary, suffered under Pontius Pilate, was crucified; died, and was buried. He descended into Hell; the third day He arose again from the dead; He ascended into Heaven, sitteth at the right hand of God, the Father Almighty; from thence He shall come to judge the living and the dead.

I believe in the Holy Ghost, the Holy Catholic Church, the communion of Saints, the forgiveness of sins, the resurrection of the body, and the life everlasting. Amen.

The Confiteor

I confess to Almighty God, to Blessed Mary, ever Virgin, to Blessed Michael the Archangel, to Blessed John the Baptist, to the Holy Apostles Peter and Paul, and to all the Saints, that I have sinned exceedingly in thought, word and deed, through my fault, through my fault, through my most grievous fault. Therefore, I beseech Blessed Mary, ever Virgin, Blessed Michael the Archangel, Blessed John the Baptist, the Holy Apostles Peter and Paul, and all the Saints, to pray to the Lord our God for me.

May the Almighty God have mercy on me, and forgive me my sins, and bring me to everlasting life. Amen.

May the Almighty and merciful Lord grant me pardon, absolution and remission of all my sins. Amen.

An Act of Faith

O my God! I firmly believe that Thou art one God in three Divine Persons, Father, Son, and Holy Ghost; I believe that Thy Divine Son became man, and died for our sins, and that He will come to judge the living and the dead. I believe these and all the truths which the Holy Catholic Church teaches, because Thou hast revealed them, who canst neither deceive nor be deceived.

An Act of Hope

O my God! Relying on Thy infinite goodness and promises, I hope to obtain pardon of my sins, the help of Thy grace, and life everlasting, through the merits of Jesus Christ, my Lord and Redeemer.

An Act of Love

O my God! I love Thee above all things, with my whole heart and soul, because Thou art all-good and worthy of all love. I love my neighbor as myself for the love of Thee. I forgive all who have injured me, and ask pardon of all whom I have injured.

An Act of Contrition

O my God! I am heartily sorry for having offended Thee, and I detest all my sins, because I dread the loss of Heaven and the pains of Hell, but most of all because they offend Thee, my God, who art all-good and deserving of all my love. I firmly resolve, with the help of Thy grace, to confess my sins, to do penance, and to amend my life.

The Blessing before Meals

✠ Bless us, O Lord! and these Thy gifts, which we are about to receive from Thy bounty, through Christ Our Lord. Amen.

Grace after Meals

✠ We give Thee thanks for all Thy benefits, O Almighty God, who livest and reignest forever; and may the souls of the faithful departed through the mercy of God, rest in peace. Amen.

The Manner in Which a Lay Person Is to Baptize in Case of Necessity

Pour common water on the head or face of the person to be baptized, and say while pouring it:

"I baptize thee in the name of the Father, and of the Son, and of the Holy Ghost."

N.B. Any person of either sex who has reached the use of reason can baptize in case of necessity, but the same person must say the words while pouring the water.

CATECHISM

KEY TO PRONUNCIATION

ā	as in face	ĕ	as in edge	ū	as in huge
ȃ	as in chocolate	ẽ	as in baker	ŭ	as in up
â	as in dare	ī	as in like	û	as in burn
ă	as in act	ĭ	as in fin	o͞o	as in mood
ä	as in farm	ō	as in old	o͝o	as in brook
ȧ	as in tall	ô	as in or	ou	as in out
ē	as in eve	ŏ	as in oft		

LESSON FIRST

On the End of Man

A-pos′tles (ȧ-pŏs′′lz), the twelve men chosen by Christ to carry on His work.

Chief (chēf), the most important.

Com-posed′ (kŏm-pōzd′), made up of.

Cre-a′tor (krē-ā′tẽr), the One who made all things out of nothing.

Crea′ture (krē′tūr), everything made by God out of nothing.

Creed (krēd), a list of the principal truths of faith in a few words.

Cru′ci-fied (krū′sĭ-fīd), nailed hands and feet to a cross.

End, the purpose for which he was made.

Ev′er-last′ing (ĕv′ẽr-lăst′ĭng), that never comes to an end.

Free will, power to choose the right or wrong.

Know, to learn all we can about.

Serve (sẽrv), to do His holy will.

Soul, the spirit in man giving life to the body.

Spir′it (spĭr′ĭt), a living being which cannot be seen or touched.

Un′der-stand′ing (ŭn′dẽr-stănd′-ĭng), the power of knowing right from wrong.

Wor′ship (wûr′shĭp), to pay God the honor due Him alone, to adore.

1. Q. Who made the world?

A. God made the world.

2. Q. Who is God?

A. God is the Creator of heaven and earth, and of all things.

3. Q. What is man?

A. Man is a creature composed of body and soul, and made to the image and likeness of God.

4. **Q. Is this likeness in the body or in the soul?**
   A. This likeness is chiefly in the soul.

5. **Q. How is the soul like to God?**
   A. The soul is like God because it is a spirit that will never die, and has understanding and free will.

6. **Q. Why did God make you?**
   A. God made me to know Him, to love Him, and to serve Him in this world, and to be happy with Him forever in the next.

7. **Q. Of which must we take more care, our soul or our body?**
   A. We must take more care of our soul than of our body.

8. **Q. Why must we take more care of our soul than of our body?**
   A. We must take more care of our soul than of our body, because in losing our soul we lose God and everlasting happiness.

9. **Q. What must we do to save our souls?**
   A. To save our souls we must worship God by faith, hope, and charity; that is, we must believe in Him, hope in Him, and love Him with all our heart.

10. **Q. How shall we know the things which we are to believe?**
   A. We shall know the things which we are to believe from the Catholic Church, through which God speaks to us.

11. **Q. Where shall we find the chief truths which the Church teaches?**
   A. We shall find the chief truths which the Church teaches in the Apostles' Creed.

12. Q. Say the Apostles' Creed.

A. I believe in God, the Father Almighty, Creator of heaven and earth; and in Jesus Christ, His only Son, our Lord; who was conceived by the Holy Ghost, born of the Virgin Mary, suffered under Pontius Pilate, was crucified; died, and was buried. He descended into Hell; the third day He arose again from the dead; He ascended into Heaven, and sitteth at the right hand of God, the Father Almighty; from thence He shall come to judge the living and the dead. I believe in the Holy Ghost, the Holy Catholic Church, the communion of Saints, the forgiveness of sins, the resurrection of the body, and the life everlasting. Amen.

LESSON SECOND

On God and His Perfections

Im-pos´si-ble (ĭm-pŏs´ĭ-b'l), can not be done.

In´fi-nite-ly (ĭn´fĭ-nĭt-lĭ), beyond measure.

Mer´ci-ful (mẽr´sĭ-fŭl), kind, and forgiving.

Per´fect (pẽr´fekt), so good that nothing can be better.

Per-fec´tions (pẽr-fĕk´shŭnz), good qualities.

Se´cret (sē´krĕt), that which is known to myself only.

13. Q. What is God?

A. God is a spirit infinitely perfect.

14. Q. Had God a beginning?

A. God had no beginning; He always was and He always will be.

15. Q. Where is God?

A. God is everywhere.

16. Q. If God is everywhere, why do we not see Him?

A. We do not see God, because He is a pure spirit and cannot be seen with bodily eyes.

17. Q. Does God see us?

A. God sees us and watches over us.

18. Q. Does God know all things?

A. God knows all things, even our most secret thoughts, words, and actions.

19. Q. Can God do all things?

A. God can do all things, and nothing is hard or impossible to Him.

20. Q. Is God just, holy, and merciful?

A. God is all just, all holy, all merciful, as He is infinitely perfect.

LESSON THIRD

On the Unity and Trinity of God

Dis-tinct′ (dĭs-tĭnkt′), separate, different.
Di-vine′ (dĭ-vīn′), having the nature of God.
Di-vine′ Na′ture (nā′tūr), that which is one in God.
E′qual (ē′kwăl), another just as great and perfect as Himself.
In′fi-nite (ĭn′fĭ-nĭt), without limit.
Sub′stance (sŭb′stăns), the very heart of a thing.
Su-preme′ (sū-prēm′), above all.
Trin′i-ty (trĭn′ĭ-tĭ), three in one.
U′ni-ty (ū′nĭ-tĭ), being only one.

21. Q. Is there but one God?
A. Yes; there is but one God.

22. Q. Why can there be but one God?
A. There can be but one God, because God, being supreme and infinite, cannot have an equal.

23. Q. How many Persons are there in God?
A. In God there are three Divine Persons, really distinct, and equal in all things—the Father, the Son, and the Holy Ghost.

24. Q. Is the Father God?
A. The Father is God and the first Person of the Blessed Trinity.

25. Q. Is the Son God?

A. The Son is God and the second Person of the Blessed Trinity.

26. Q. Is the Holy Ghost God?

A. The Holy Ghost is God and the third Person of the Blessed Trinity.

27. Q. What do you mean by the Blessed Trinity?

A. By the Blessed Trinity I mean one God in three Divine Persons.

28. Q. Are the three Divine Persons equal in all things?

A. The three Divine Persons are equal in all things.

29. Q. Are the three Divine Persons one and the same God?

A. The three Divine Persons are one and the same God, having one and the same Divine Nature and substance.

30. Q. Can we fully understand how the three Divine Persons are one and the same God?

A. We cannot fully understand how the three Divine Persons are one and the same God, because this is a mystery.

31. Q. What is a mystery?

A. A mystery is a truth which we cannot fully understand.

LESSON FOURTH

On Creation

Ap-point´ed (ă-point´ed), named to the position.

As-sist´ (ă-sĭst´), to stand, to be in readiness.

Cre-at´ed (krē-āt´ĕd), made, as God alone can make, out of nothing.

Guard´i-an (gär´dĭ-ăn), one who is given the care and protection of another.

Min´is-ter (mĭn´ĭs-tēr), to attend upon and serve.

Pur´pose (pûr´pŭs), the reason one has for doing a thing.

32. Q. Who created Heaven and earth, and all things?

A. God created Heaven and earth, and all things.

33. Q. How did God create Heaven and earth?

A. God created Heaven and earth from nothing by His word only; that is, by a single act of His all-powerful will.

34. Q. Which are the chief creatures of God?

A. The chief creatures of God are angels and men.

35. Q. What are angels?

A. Angels are pure spirits without a body, created to adore and enjoy God in Heaven.

36. Q. Were the angels created for any other purpose?

A. The angels were also created to assist before the throne of God and to minister unto Him; they have often been sent as messengers from God to man; and are also appointed our guardians.

37. Q. Were the angels, as God created them, good and happy?

A. The angels, as God created them, were good and happy.

38. Q. Did all the angels remain good and happy?

A. All the angels did not remain good and happy; many of them sinned and were cast into Hell, and these are called devils or bad angels.

LESSON FIFTH

On Our First Parents And the Fall

Be-fell′ (bē-fĕl′), happened to.

Con-cep′tion (kŏn-sĕp′shŭn), joining of soul and body at the beginning of life.

Con′stant (kŏn′stănt), going steadily on without change.

Cor-rupt′ed (kŏ-rŭpt′ĕd), spoiled, weakened.

Doomed (do͞omd), condemned.

Ef-fects′ (ĕ-fĕkts′), results.

E′vil (ē′v′l), misfortune, harm.

Faith′ful (fāth′fŭl), true, steady in obedience.

Glo′ry (glō′rĭ), the delight of looking at God in Heaven.

Guilt (gĭlt), stain, taint.

Im-mac′u-late (ĭ-măk′ū-lȧt), not stained by sin of any kind.

In′cli-na′tion (ĭn′klĭ-nā′shŭn), a liking for.

In-her′it (ĭn-hĕr′ĭt), to come into possession of through our parents or by a will.

In′no-cent (ĭn′ō-sĕnt), free from all sin.

Mer′its (mĕr′ĭts), what Jesus won by the Redemption.

O-rig′i-nal (ō-rĭj′ĭ-năl), the first, from which the others flow.

Our nature, that in us by which we can know what is right and choose what is good.

Par′a-dise (păr′ȧ-dīs), the place where Adam and Eve first lived.

Pre-served′ (prē-zûrvd′), kept free from, excepted from.

Priv′i-lege (prĭv′ĭ-lĕj), exceptional favor.

Pun′ish-ment (pŭn′ĭsh-mĕnt), suffering, sent on them by God.

Try (trī), to put to the test or trial

39. Q. Who were the first man and woman?

A. The first man and woman were Adam and Eve.

40. Q. Were Adam and Eve innocent and holy when they came from the hand of God?

A. Adam and Eve were innocent and holy when they came from the hand of God.

41. Q. Did God give any command to Adam and Eve?

A. To try their obedience God commanded Adam and Eve not to eat of a certain fruit which grew in the garden of Paradise.

42. Q. Which were the chief blessings intended for Adam and Eve had they remained faithful to God?

A. The chief blessings intended for Adam and Eve, had they remained faithful to God, were a constant state of happiness in this life and everlasting glory in the next.

43. Q. Did Adam and Eve remain faithful to God?

A. Adam and Eve did not remain faithful to God; but broke His command by eating the forbidden fruit.

44. Q. What befell Adam and Eve on account of their sin?

A. Adam and Eve, on account of their sin, lost innocence and holiness, and were doomed to sickness and death.

45. Q. What evil befell us on account of the disobedience of our first parents?

A. On account of the disobedience of our first parents, we all share in their sin and punishment, as we should have shared in their happiness if they had remained faithful.

46. Q. What other effects followed from the sin of our first parents?

A. Our nature was corrupted by the sin of our first parents, which darkened our understanding, weakened our will, and left in us a strong inclination to evil.

47. Q. What is the sin called which we inherit from our first parents?

A. The sin which we inherit from our first parents is called Original Sin.

48. Q. Why is this sin called Original?

A. This sin is called Original because it comes down to us from our first parents, and we are brought into the world with its guilt on our soul.

49. Q. Does this corruption of our nature remain in us after Original Sin is forgiven?

A. This corruption of our nature and other punishments remain in us after Original Sin is forgiven.

50. Q. Was any one ever preserved from Original Sin?

A. The Blessed Virgin Mary, through the merits of her Divine Son, was preserved free from the guilt of Original Sin, and this privilege is called her Immaculate Conception.

LESSON SIXTH

On Sin and Its Kinds

Ac′tu-al (ăk′tū-ăl), real, relating to our own acts.
Cap′i-tal (kăp′ĭ-tăl), the heads, the sources of others.
Con-sent′ (kŏn-sĕnt′), giving in to.
Cov′et-ous-ness (kŭv′ĕ-tŭs-nĕs), too great a desire for money or goods.
Dam-na′tion (dăm-nā′shŭn), casting into Hell.
En′vy (ĕn′vĭ), sadness at another's welfare.
Glut′ton-y (glŭt′′nĭ), eating or drinking too much.
Grace (grās), God's work in our soul.
Griev′ous (grēv′ŭs), very great.
Lust (lŭst), strong desire for impure thoughts, words, or actions.
Mat′ter (măt′ĕr), the act done.
Mor′tal (môr′tăl), that which kills; deadly.
Of-fense′ (ŏ-fĕns′), failing, disobedience.
O-mis′sion (ō-mĭsh′ŭn), the leaving out of a duty.
Pride (prīd), taking credit to ourselves for what was given us by God.
Re-flec′tion (rē-flĕk′shŭn), thinking a thing over.
Re-sist′ (rē-zĭst′), to refuse to do.
Sanc′ti-fy-ing (sănk′tĭ-fī-ĭng), making holy or pleasing to God.
Sloth (slŏth), laziness which keeps us from doing our duty.
Spir′i-tu-al (spĭr′ĭ-tū-ăl), belonging to the soul.
Suf-fi′cient (sŭ-fĭsh′ĕnt), enough to know whether it is right or wrong.
Ve′ni-al (vē′nĭ-ăl), more easily forgiven.
Will′ful (wĭl′fŭl), done on purpose.

51. Q. Is Original Sin the only kind of sin?

A. Original Sin is not the only kind of sin; there is another kind of sin, which we commit ourselves, called actual sin.

52. Q. **What is actual sin?**

A. Actual sin is any willful thought, word, deed, or omission contrary to the law of God.

53. Q. **How many kinds of actual sin are there?**

A. There are two kinds of actual sin—mortal and venial.

54. Q. **What is mortal sin?**

A. Mortal sin is a grievous offense against the law of God.

55. Q. **Why is this sin called mortal?**

A. This sin is called mortal because it deprives us of spiritual life, which is sanctifying grace, and brings everlasting death and damnation on the soul.

56. Q. **How many things are necessary to make a sin mortal?**

A. To make a sin mortal three things are necessary: a grievous matter, sufficient reflection, and full consent of the will.

57. Q. **What is venial sin?**

A. Venial sin is a slight offense against the law of God in matters of less importance, or in matters of great importance it is an offense committed without sufficient reflection or full consent of the will.

58. Q. **Which are the effects of venial sin?**

A. The effects of venial sin are the lessening of the love of God in our heart, the making us less worthy of His help, and the weakening of the power to resist mortal sin.

59. Q. **Which are the chief sources of sin?**

A. The chief sources of sin are seven: Pride, Covetousness, Lust, Anger, Gluttony, Envy, and Sloth; and they are commonly called capital sins.

LESSON SEVENTH

On the Incarnation and Redemption

A-ban′don (ȧ-băn′dŭn), to leave one helpless.

An-nun′ci-a′tion (ă-nŭn′-sē-ā′-shŭn), the making known, announcing—March 25.

Con-ceived′ (kŏn-sēvd′), given life to.

E-ter′ni-ty (ē-tĕr′nĭ-tĭ), always, forever.

Im-me′di-ate′ly (ĭ-mē′dĭ-ât′lĭ), without delay.

In′car-na′tion (ĭn′kär-nā′shŭn), the act of becoming man.

Man′kind (măn′kīnd), all the people of the world.

Re-deem′er (rē-dē′mĕr), the One who was to deliver man from the slavery of sin.

Re-demp′tion (rē-dĕmp′shŭn), the deliverance from sin and its punishment by the death of Christ.

Sat′is-fy (săt′ĭs-fī), pay in full for.

60. Q. Did God abandon man after he fell into sin?

A. God did not abandon man after he fell into sin, but promised him a Redeemer, who was to satisfy for man's sin and reopen to him the gates of Heaven.

61. Q. Who is the Redeemer?

A. Our Blessed Lord and Saviour Jesus Christ is the Redeemer of mankind.

62. Q. What do you believe of Jesus Christ?

A. I believe that Jesus Christ is the Son of God, the second Person of the Blessed Trinity, true God and true man.

63. Q. Why is Jesus Christ true God?

A. Jesus Christ is true God because He is the true and only Son of God the Father.

64. Q. Why is Jesus Christ true man?

A. Jesus Christ is true man because He is the Son of the Blessed Virgin Mary and has a body and soul like ours.

65. Q. How many natures are there in Jesus Christ?

A. In Jesus Christ there are two natures, the nature of God and the nature of man.

66. Q. Is Jesus Christ more than one person?

A. No, Jesus Christ is but one Divine Person.

67. Q. Was Jesus Christ always God?

A. Jesus Christ was always God, as He is the second Person of the Blessed Trinity, equal to His Father from all eternity.

68. Q. Was Jesus Christ always man?

A. Jesus Christ was not always man, but became man at the time of His Incarnation.

69. Q. What do you mean by the Incarnation?

A. By the Incarnation I mean that the Son of God was made man.

70. Q. How was the Son of God made man?

A. The Son of God was conceived and made man by the power of the Holy Ghost, in the womb of the Blessed Virgin Mary.

71. Q. Is the Blessed Virgin Mary truly the Mother of God?

A. The Blessed Virgin Mary is truly the Mother of God, because the same Divine Person who is the Son of God is also the Son of the Blessed Virgin Mary.

72. Q. **Did the Son of God become man immediately after the sin of our first parents?**

A. The Son of God did not become man immediately after the sin of our first parents, but was promised to them as a Redeemer.

73. Q. **How could they be saved who lived before the Son of God became man?**

A. They who lived before the Son of God became man could be saved by believing in a Redeemer to come, and by keeping the Commandments.

74. Q. **On what day was the Son of God conceived and made man?**

A. The Son of God was conceived and made man on Annunciation day—the day on which the Angel Gabriel announced to the Blessed Virgin Mary that she was to be the Mother of God,

75. Q. **On what day was Christ born?**

A. Christ was born on Christmas day in a stable at Bethlehem, over nineteen hundred years ago.

76. Q. **How long did Christ live on earth?**

A. Christ lived on earth about thirty-three years, and led a most holy life in poverty and suffering.

77. Q. **Why did Christ live so long on earth?**

A. Christ lived so long on earth to show us the way to Heaven by His teachings and example.

LESSON EIGHTH

On Our Lord's Passion, Death, Resurrection, and Ascension

Al-might′y (ôl-mīt′ĭ), all powerful.

As-cen′sion (ă-sĕn′shŭn), the act of going up into Heaven.

Cal′va-ry (kăl′vȧ-rĭ), a hill outside Jerusalem.

Damned (dămd), the spirits and souls lost forever.

De-scend′ed (dē-sĕn′dĕd), went down.

Glo′ri-ous (glō′rĭ-ŭs), bright, shining.

Im-mor′tal (ĭ-môr′tăl), never to die.

Lim′bo (lĭm′bō), a place of rest.

Pas′sion (păsh′ŭn), the last great sufferings of our Saviour.

Pur′chased (pûr′châst), bought with a price.

Res′ur-rec′tion (rĕz′ŭ-rĕk′shŭn), the rising again from the dead.

Right hand, in the place of honor.

Sat′is-fy′ing (săt′ĭs-fī′ĭng), paying all claims.

Scourg′ing (skûrj′ĭng), lashing with a whip.

Sep′ul-chre (sĕp′ŭl-kēr), the place where a body lies buried.

Ti′dings (tī′dĭngz), news.

78. Q. What did Jesus Christ suffer?

A. Jesus Christ suffered a bloody sweat, a cruel scourging, was crowned with thorns, and was crucified.

79. Q. On what day did Christ die?

A. Christ died on Good Friday.

80. Q. Why do you call that day "good" on which Christ died so sorrowful a death?

A. We call that day "good" on which Christ died because by His death He showed His great love for man, and purchased for him every blessing,

81. Q. Where did Christ die?

A. Christ died on Mount Calvary.

82. Q. How did Christ die?

A. Christ was nailed to the Cross and died on it between two thieves.

83. Q. Why did Christ suffer and die?

A. Christ suffered and died for our sins.

84. Q. What lessons do we learn from the sufferings and death of Christ?

A. From the sufferings and death of Christ we learn the great evil of sin, the hatred God bears to it, and the necessity of satisfying for it.

85. Q. Whither did Christ's soul go after His death?

A. After Christ's death His soul descended into hell.

86. Q. Did Christ's soul descend into the hell of the damned?

A. The hell into which Christ's soul descended was not the hell of the damned, but a place or state of rest called Limbo, where the souls of the just were waiting for Him.

87. Q. Why did Christ descend into Limbo?

A. Christ descended into Limbo to preach to the souls who were in prison—that is, to announce to them the joyful tidings of their redemption.

88. Q. Where was Christ's body while His soul was in Limbo?

A. While Christ's soul was in Limbo His body was in the holy sepulchre.

89. Q. On what day did Christ rise from the dead?

A. Christ rose from the dead, glorious and immortal, on Easter Sunday, the third day after His death.

90. Q. How long did Christ stay on earth after His resurrection?

A. Christ stayed on earth forty days after His resurrection to show that He was truly risen from the dead, and to instruct His Apostles.

91. Q. After Christ had remained forty days on earth whither did He go?

A. After forty days Christ ascended into Heaven, and the day on which He ascended into Heaven is called Ascension day.

92. Q. Where is Christ in Heaven?

A. In Heaven Christ sits at the right hand of God the Father Almighty.

93. Q. What do you mean by saying that Christ sits at the right hand of God?

A. When I say that Christ sits at the right hand of God I mean that Christ as God is equal to His Father in all things, and that as man He is in the highest place in Heaven next to God.

LESSON NINTH

On the Holy Ghost and His Descent upon the Apostles

A-bide′ (ȧ-bīd′), to stay or remain.
En-a′ble (ĕn-ā′b'l), to make able.
En-light′en (ĕn-līt′′n), to make them understand better
Pen′te-cost (pĕn′tĕ-kŏst), the fiftieth day after Easter.
Pro-ceed′ (prō-sēd′), to go forth from.
Whit′sun-day (hwĭt′s'n-dā), white Sunday.

94. Q. Who is the Holy Ghost?
A. The Holy Ghost is the third Person of the Blessed Trinity.

95. Q. From whom does the Holy Ghost proceed?
A. The Holy Ghost proceeds from the Father and the Son.

96. Q. Is the Holy Ghost equal to the Father and the Son?
A. The Holy Ghost is equal to the Father and the Son, being the same Lord and God as They are.

97. Q. On what day did the Holy Ghost come down upon the Apostles?
A. The Holy Ghost came down upon the Apostles ten days after the Ascension of Our Lord; and the day on which He came down upon the Apostles is called Whitsunday, or Pentecost.

98. Q. **How did the Holy Ghost come down upon the Apostles?**
A. The Holy Ghost came down upon the Apostles in the form of tongues of fire.

99. Q. **Who sent the Holy Ghost upon the Apostles?**
A. Our Lord Jesus Christ sent the Holy Ghost upon the Apostles.

100. Q. **Why did Christ send the Holy Ghost?**
A. Christ sent the Holy Ghost to sanctify His Church, to enlighten and strengthen the Apostles, and to enable them to preach the Gospel.

101. Q. **Will the Holy Ghost abide with the Church forever?**
A. The Holy Ghost will abide with the Church forever, and guide it in the way of holiness and truth.

LESSON TENTH

On the Effects of the Redemption

Be-stowed′ (bē-stōd′), given as a favor.

E-ter′nal (ē-tĕr′năl) **life**, the never-ending happiness of Heaven.

Mer′its (mĕr′ĭts), the rewards earned by His sufferings and death.

Neigh′bor (nā′bĕr), every one in the world.

Par-tic′u-lar (pär-tĭk′ū-lár), special.

Per′se-ver′ance (pĕr′sĕ-vēr′ăns), continuing to the end.

Re-vealed′ (rē-vēld′), made known by God.

Sal-va′tion (săl-vā′shŭn), the saving of our soul.

Shun (shŭn), to keep clear of, avoid.

State of grace, the condition of one in whose soul God dwells.

Su′per-nat′u-ral (sū′pĕr-năt′ū-răl), above nature.

Trust (trŭst), to look for confidently.

Vir′tues (vûr′tūz), habits of doing good.

102. Q. Which are the chief effects of the Redemption?

A. The chief effects of the Redemption are two: The satisfaction of God's justice by Christ's sufferings and death, and the gaining of grace for men.

103. Q. What do you mean by grace?

A. By grace I mean a supernatural gift of God bestowed on us, through the merits of Jesus Christ, for our salvation.

104. Q. How many kinds of grace are there?

A. There are two kinds of grace—sanctifying grace and actual grace.

105. Q. What is sanctifying grace?

A. Sanctifying grace is that grace which makes the soul holy and pleasing to God.

106. Q. What do you call those graces or gifts of God by which we believe in Him, hope in Him, and love Him?

A. Those graces or gifts of God by which we believe in Him, and hope in Him, and love Him, are called the Divine virtues of Faith, Hope, and Charity.

107. Q. What is Faith?

A. Faith is a Divine virtue by which we firmly believe the truths which God has revealed.

108. Q. What is Hope?

A. Hope is a Divine virtue by which we firmly trust that God will give us eternal life and the means to obtain it.

109. Q. What is Charity?

A. Charity is a Divine virtue by which we love God above all things for His own sake, and our neighbor as ourselves for the love of God.

110. Q. What is actual grace?

A. Actual grace is that help of God which enlightens our mind and moves our will to shun evil and do good.

111. Q. Is grace necessary to salvation?

A. Grace is necessary to salvation, because without grace we can do nothing to merit Heaven.

112. Q. Can we resist the grace of God?

A. We can and unfortunately often do resist the grace of God.

113. Q. What is the grace of perseverance?

A. The grace of perseverance is a particular gift of God which enables us to continue in the state of grace till death.

LESSON ELEVENTH

On the Church

Cath′o-lic (kăth′ō-lĭk), spread all over the world, universal.

Con′gre-ga′-tion (kŏn′grĕ-gā′shŭn), a union of people, a society.

Found (found), to begin or establish.

Fruits (frūts), benefits, results.

In′sti-tut′-ed (ĭn′stĭ-tūt′ĕd), given or appointed.

In-vis′i-ble (ĭn-vĭz′ĭ-b'l), that which cannot be seen.

Law′ful (lô′fŭl), by right, according to the Church's laws.

Means (mēnz), aids, helps.

Par-take′ (pär-tāk′) **of**, to receive, share in.

Pro-fess′ (prō-fĕs′), to let it be known publicly.

Suc-ces′sor (sŭk-sĕs′ĕr), one who follows in the place of another.

Vic′ar (vĭk′ĕr), a person acting in the name and with the authority of another.

Vis′i-ble (vĭz′ĭ-b'l), that which can be seen.

114. Q. Which are the means instituted by Our Lord to enable men at all times to share in the fruits of the Redemption?

A. The means instituted by Our Lord to enable men at all times to share in the fruits of His Redemption are the Church and the Sacraments.

115. Q. What is the Church?

A. The Church is the congregation of all those who profess the faith of Christ, partake of the same Sacraments, and are governed by their lawful pastors under one visible head.

116. Q. Who is the invisible Head of the Church?

A. Jesus Christ is the invisible Head of the Church.

117. Q. Who is the visible Head of the Church?

A. Our Holy Father the Pope, the Bishop of Rome, is the Vicar of Christ on earth and the visible Head of the Church.

118. Q. Why is the Pope, the Bishop of Rome, the visible Head of the Church?

A. The Pope, the Bishop of Rome, is the visible Head of the Church because he is the successor of St. Peter, whom Christ made the chief of the Apostles and the visible Head of the Church.

119. Q. Who are the successors of the other Apostles?

A. The successors of the other Apostles are the Bishops of the Holy Catholic Church.

120. Q. Why did Christ found the Church?

A. Christ founded the Church to teach, govern, sanctify, and save all men.

121. Q. Are all bound to belong to the Church?

A. All are bound to belong to the Church, and he who knows the Church to be the true Church and remains out of it cannot be saved.

LESSON TWELFTH

On the Attributes and Marks of the Church

Ap´os-tol´ic (ăp´ŏs-tŏl´ĭk), coming down from the Apostles.

At´tri-butes (ă´trĭ-būts), qualities.

De-rives´ (dē-rīvz´), gets or receives.

Doc´trine (dŏk´trĭn), a truth taught by the Church.

Em´i-nent (ĕm´ĭ-nĕnt), very great and noticeable.

Err (ûr), make a mistake.

Faith´ful (fāth´fŭl), Catholics all over the world.

In´de-fect´i-bil´i-ty (ĭn´dē-fĕk´tĭ-bĭl´ĭ-tĭ), quality of being free from decay.

In-fal´li-bil´i-ty (ĭn-făl´ĭ-bĭl´ĭ-tĭ), quality of not being able to make a mistake.

Main-tains´ (mān-tānz´), holds to and defends.

Mor´als (mōr´ălz), the right and wrong in conduct.

One com-mun´ion (kŏ-mūn´-yŭn), sharing in the same spiritual goods.

Pro-claims´ (prō-klāmz´), makes known officially.

Sub-sists´ (sŭb-sĭsts´) lives on.

122. Q. Which are the attributes of the Church?

A. The attributes of the Church are three: authority, infallibility, and indefectibility.

123. Q. What do you mean by the authority of the Church?

A. By the authority of the Church I mean the right and power which the Pope and the Bishops, as the successors of the Apostles, have to teach and to govern the faithful.

124. Q. What do you mean by the infallibility of the Church?

A. By the infallibility of the Church I mean that the Church cannot err when it teaches a doctrine of faith or morals.

125. Q. When does the Church teach infallibly?

A. The Church teaches infallibly when it speaks through the Pope and the Bishops, united in general council, or through the Pope alone when he proclaims to all the faithful a doctrine of faith or morals.

126. Q. What do you mean by the indefectibility of the Church?

A. By the indefectibility of the Church I mean that the Church, as Christ founded it, will last till the end of time.

127. Q. In whom are these attributes found in their fullness?

A. These attributes are found in their fullness in the Pope, the visible Head of the Church, whose infallible authority to teach bishops, priests, and people in matters of faith or morals will last till the end of the world.

128. Q. Has the Church any marks by which it may be known?

A. The Church has four marks by which it may be known: it is One; it is Holy; it is Catholic; it is Apostolic.

129. Q. How is the Church One?

A. The Church is One because all its members agree in one faith, are all in one communion, and are all under one Head.

130. Q. How is the Church Holy?

A. The Church is Holy because its founder, Jesus Christ, is holy; because it teaches a holy doctrine; invites all to a holy life; and because of the eminent holiness of so many thousands of its children.

131. Q. How is the Church Catholic or universal?

A. The Church is Catholic or universal because it subsists in all ages, teaches all nations, and maintains all truth.

132. Q. How is the Church Apostolic?

A. The Church is Apostolic because it was founded by Christ on His Apostles, and is governed by their lawful successors, and because it has never ceased, and never will cease, to teach their doctrine.

133. Q. In which Church are these attributes and marks found?

A. These attributes and marks are found in the Holy Roman Catholic Church alone.

134. Q. From whom does the Church derive its undying life and infallible authority?

A. The Church derives its undying life and infallible authority from the Holy Ghost, the Spirit of truth, who abides with it forever.

135. Q. By whom is the Church made and kept One, Holy, and Catholic?

A. The Church is made and kept One, Holy, and Catholic by the Holy Ghost, the Spirit of love and holiness, who unites and sanctifies its members throughout the world.

LESSON THIRTEENTH

On the Sacraments in General

At-tain′ (ă-tān′), to reach or come to.

Char′ac-ter (kăr′ăk-tẽr), mark, sta mp.

Dis′po-si′tions (dĭs′pō-zĭsh′ŭnz), state of mind and heart.

Ex-treme′ (ěks-trēm′), last.

Im-print′ (ĭm-prĭnt′), to stamp.

Out′ward (out′wẽrd), that which can be seen, heard or felt.

Sac′ra-men′tal (săk′rȧ-mĕn′tăl), belonging to a sacrament.

Sac′ri-lege (săk′rĭ-lĕj), willful abuse of or disrespect for any sacred person, place, or thing.

Sign, that which stands for something else.

Wor′thi-ly (wûr′thĭ-lĭ), in the right way.

136. Q. What is a Sacrament?

A. A Sacrament is an outward sign instituted by Christ to give grace.

137. Q. How many Sacraments are there?

A. There are seven Sacraments: Baptism, Confirmation, Holy Eucharist, Penance, Extreme Unction, Holy Orders, and Matrimony.

138. Q. Whence have the Sacraments the power of giving grace?

A. The Sacraments have the power of giving grace from the merits of Jesus Christ.

139. Q. What grace do the Sacraments give?

A. Some of the Sacraments give sanctifying grace, and others increase it in our souls.

140. Q. Which are the Sacraments that give sanctifying grace?

A. The Sacraments that give sanctifying grace are Baptism and Penance; and they are called Sacraments of the dead.

141. Q. Why are Baptism and Penance called Sacraments of the dead?

A. Baptism and Penance are called Sacraments of the dead, because they take away sin, which is the death of the soul, and give grace, which is its life.

142. Q. Which are the Sacraments that increase sanctifying grace in our soul?

A. The Sacraments that increase sanctifying grace in our soul are: Confirmation, Holy Eucharist, Extreme Unction, Holy Orders, and Matrimony; and they are called Sacraments of the living.

143. Q. Why are Confirmation, Holy Eucharist, Extreme Unction, Holy Orders, and Matrimony called Sacraments of the living?

A. Confirmation, Holy Eucharist, Extreme Unction, Holy Orders, and Matrimony are called Sacraments of the living, because those who receive them worthily are already living the life of grace.

144. Q. What sin does he commit who receives the Sacraments of the living in mortal sin?

A. He who receives the Sacraments of the living in mortal sin commits a sacrilege, which is a great sin, because it is an abuse of a sacred thing.

145. Q. Besides sanctifying grace do the Sacraments give any other grace?

A. Besides sanctifying grace the Sacraments give another grace, called sacramental.

146. Q. What is sacramental grace?

A. Sacramental grace is a special help which God gives, to attain the end for which He instituted each Sacrament.

147. Q. Do the Sacraments always give grace?

A. The Sacraments always give grace, if we receive them with the right dispositions.

148. Q. Can we receive the Sacraments more than once?

A. We can receive the Sacraments more than once, except Baptism, Confirmation, and Holy Orders.

149. Q. Why can we not receive Baptism, Confirmation, and Holy Orders more than once?

A. We cannot receive Baptism, Confirmation, and Holy Orders more than once, because they imprint a character in the soul.

150. Q. What is the character which these Sacraments imprint in the soul?

A. The character which these Sacraments imprint in the soul is a spiritual mark which remains forever.

151. Q. Does this character remain in the soul even after death?

A. This character remains in the soul even after death: for the honor and glory of those who are saved; for the shame and punishment of those who are lost.

LESSON FOURTEENTH

On Baptism

Ad-min′is-ter (ăd-mĭn′ĭs-tẽr), give or perform.
Ar′dent (är′dĕnt), very great or strong.
Cleans′es (klĕnz′ĕz), washes, frees.
Heirs (ârz), inheritors, entitled to.
Ob-li-ga′tion (ŏb-lĭ-gā′shŭn), something that one is bound to do, duty.
Or-dained′ (ôr-dānd′), ordered or commanded.
Or′di-na-ry (ôr′dĭ-nā-rĭ), usual or regular.
Pomps (pŏmps), snares or traps disguised to lead you into sin.
Re-mit′ted (rē-mĭt′ĕd), blotted out.
Re-nounce′ (rē-nouns′), give up.

152. Q. What is Baptism?
A. Baptism is a Sacrament which cleanses us from Original Sin, makes us Christians, children of God, and heirs of Heaven.

153. Q. Are actual sins ever remitted by Baptism?
A. Actual sins and all the punishment due to them are remitted by Baptism, if the person baptized be guilty of any.

154. Q. Is Baptism necessary to salvation?
A. Baptism is necessary to salvation, because without it we cannot enter into the Kingdom of Heaven.

155. Q. Who can administer Baptism?

A. The priest is the ordinary minister of Baptism; but in case of necessity any one who has the use of reason may baptize.

156. Q. How is Baptism given?

A. Whoever baptizes should pour water on the head of the person to be baptized, and say, while pouring the water: "I baptize thee in the name of the Father, and of the Son, and of the Holy Ghost."

157. Q. How many kinds of Baptism are there?

A. There are three kinds of Baptism: Baptism of water, of desire, and of blood.

158. Q. What is Baptism of water?

A. Baptism of water is that which is given by pouring water on the head of the person to be baptized, and saying at the same time: "I baptize thee in the name of the Father, and of the Son, and of the Holy Ghost."

159. Q. What is Baptism of desire?

A. Baptism of desire is an ardent wish to receive Baptism, and to do all that God has ordained for our salvation.

160. Q. What is Baptism of blood?

A. Baptism of blood is the shedding of one's blood for the faith of Christ.

161. Q. Is Baptism of desire or of blood sufficient to produce the effects of Baptism of water?

A. Baptism of desire or of blood is sufficient to produce the effects of the Baptism of water, if it is impossible to receive the Baptism of water.

162. Q. What do we promise in Baptism?

A. In Baptism we promise to renounce the devil with all his works and pomps.

163. Q. Why is the name of a saint given in Baptism?

A. The name of a saint is given in Baptism in order that the person baptized may imitate his virtues and have him for a protector.

164. Q. Why are godfathers and godmothers given in Baptism?

A. Godfathers and godmothers are given in Baptism in order that they may promise, in the name of the child, what the child itself would promise if it had the use of reason.

165. Q. What is the obligation of a godfather and a godmother?

A. The obligation of a godfather and a godmother is to instruct the child in its religious duties, if the parents neglect to do so or die.

LESSON FIFTEENTH

On Confirmation

A-noints′ (ȧ-noints′), rubs with oil.
Balm (bäm), the juice of the balsam tree.
Con-firm′ (kŏn-fûrm′), make strong.
Con′se-crat′ed (kŏn′sĕ-krāt′ĕd), blessed and so set apart as holy.
Ex-posed′ (ĕks-pōzd′), laid open, subject to.
Mys′ter-ies (mĭs′tĕr-ĭz), truths.
Na′ture (nā′tūr), meaning.
Temp-ta′tions (tĕmp-tā′shŭnz), whatever might draw one into sin.
Vi′o-lent (vī′ō-lĕnt), very strong.

166. Q. What is Confirmation?

A. Confirmation is a Sacrament through which we receive the Holy Ghost to make us strong and perfect Christians and soldiers of Jesus Christ.

167. Q. Who administers Confirmation?

A. The Bishop is the ordinary minister of Confirmation.

168. Q. How does the Bishop give Confirmation?

A. The Bishop extends his hands over those who are to be confirmed, prays that they may receive the Holy Ghost, and anoints the forehead of each with holy chrism in the form of a cross.

169. Q. What is holy chrism?

A. Holy chrism is a mixture of olive-oil and balm, consecrated by the Bishop.

170. Q. What does the Bishop say in anointing the person he confirms?

A. In anointing the person he confirms the Bishop says: "I sign thee with the sign of the cross, and I confirm thee with the chrism of salvation, in the name of the Father, and of the Son, and of the Holy Ghost."

171. Q. What is meant by anointing the forehead with chrism in the form of a cross?

A. By anointing the forehead with chrism in the form of a cross is meant, that the Christian who is confirmed must openly profess and practice his faith, never be ashamed of it, and rather die than deny it.

172. Q. Why does the Bishop give the person he confirms a slight blow on the cheek?

A. The Bishop gives the person he confirms a slight blow on the cheek, to put him in mind that he must be ready to suffer everything, even death, for the sake of Christ.

173. Q. To receive Confirmation worthily is it necessary to be in the state of grace?

A. To receive Confirmation worthily it is necessary to be in the state of grace.

174. Q. What special preparation should be made to receive Confirmation?

A. Persons of an age to learn should know the chief mysteries of faith and the duties of a Christian, and be instructed in the nature and effects of this Sacrament.

175. Q. Is it a sin to neglect Confirmation?

A. It is a sin to neglect Confirmation, especially in these evil days when faith and morals are exposed to so many and such violent temptations.

LESSON SIXTEENTH

On the Gifts and Fruits of the Holy Ghost

Be-at′i-tudes (bē-ăt′ĭ-tūdz), blessings—part of Our Lord's Sermon on the Mount on blessedness.

Be-nig′ni-ty (bĕ-nĭg′nĭ-tĭ), kindness and sweetness.

Char′i-ty, love of God and of neighbor.

Clean of Heart, persons whose thoughts are pure and holy.

Con′ti-nen-cy (kŏn′tĭ-nĕn-sĭ), self-control.

De-ceits′ (dē-sēts′), frauds, snares.

Filled (fĭld), that is, with grace and goodness.

Fruits, the things produced by the gifts.

Joy, pleasure in doing God's Will.

Jus′tice (jŭs′tĭs), goodness, virtue.

Long′-suf-fer-ing (lŏng′ sŭf-ĕr-ĭng), patience that never grows tired.

Meek (mēk), gentle, sweet-tempered.

Mourn, grieve for their sins and for Christ's sufferings.

Per′se-cu′tion (pûr′sĕ-kū′shŭn), injury or annoyance from others on account of our religion.

Poor in spir′it, valuing the things of God more than the things of the world.

Rel′ish (rĕl′ĭsh), taste or liking for.

176. Q. Which are the effects of Confirmation?

A. The effects of Confirmation are an increase of sanctifying grace, the strengthening of our faith, and the gifts of the Holy Ghost.

177. Q. Which are the gifts of the Holy Ghost?

A. The gifts of the Holy Ghost are Wisdom, Understanding, Counsel, Fortitude, Knowledge, Piety and Fear of the Lord.

178. Q. Why do we receive the gift of Fear of the Lord?

A. We receive the gift of Fear of the Lord to fill us with a dread of sin.

179. Q. Why do we receive the gift of Piety?

A. We receive the gift of Piety to make us love God as a Father and obey Him because we love Him.

180. Q. Why do we receive the gift of Knowledge?

A. We receive the gift of Knowledge to enable us to discover the Will of God in all things.

181. Q. Why do we receive the gift of Fortitude?

A. We receive the gift of Fortitude to strengthen us to do the Will of God in all things.

182. Q. Why do we receive the gift of Counsel?

A. We receive the gift of Counsel to warn us of the deceits of the devil, and of the dangers to salvation.

183. Q. Why do we receive the gift of Understanding?

A. We receive the gift of Understanding to enable us to know more clearly the mysteries of faith.

184. Q. Why do we receive the gift of Wisdom?

A. We receive the gift of Wisdom to give us a relish for the things of God, and to direct our whole life and all our actions to His honor and glory.

185. Q. Which are the Beatitudes?

A. The Beatitudes are:

1. Blessed are the poor in spirit, for theirs is the Kingdom of Heaven.
2. Blessed are the meek, for they shall possess the land.
3. Blessed are they that mourn, for they shall be comforted.
4. Blessed are they that hunger and thirst after justice, for they shall be filled.

5. Blessed are the merciful, for they shall obtain mercy.
6. Blessed are the clean of heart, for they shall see God.
7. Blessed are the peacemakers, for they shall be called the children of God.
8. Blessed are they that suffer persecution for justice's sake, for theirs is the Kingdom of Heaven.

186. Q. Which are the twelve fruits of the Holy Ghost?

A. The twelve fruits of the Holy Ghost are Charity, Joy, Peace, Patience, Benignity, Goodness, Long-suffering, Mildness, Faith, Modesty, Continency, and Chastity.

LESSON SEVENTEENTH

On the Sacrament of Penance

Ab′so-lu′tion (ăb′sō-lū′shŭn), pardon given in Christ's name.

Ab-solv′ing (ăb-zŏlv′ĭng), taking away sin.

Con′science (kŏn′shĕns), that within us which tells us when we do wrong.

De-test′ (dē-tĕst′), to hate.

Ear′nest (ûr′nĕst) **effort**, doing our very best.

Ex-am′ine (ĕg-zăm′ĭn), to ask questions of ourselves.

Firm, that cannot be shaken.

Pre′cepts (prē′sĕpts), commandments.

Re-mit′ (rē-mĭt′), forgive.

Res′o-lu′tion (rĕz′ō-lū′shŭn) making up our mind.

Re-store′ (rē-stôr′), to give back.

Re-tain′ (rē-tān′), to refuse to forgive; to hold.

Wor′thy (wûr′thĭ), good.

187. Q. What is the Sacrament of Penance?

A. Penance is a Sacrament in which the sins committed after Baptism are forgiven.

188. Q. How does the Sacrament of Penance remit sin, and restore to the soul the friendship of God?

A. The Sacrament of Penance remits sins and restores the friendship of God to the soul by means of the absolution of the priest.

189. Q. How do you know that the priest has the power of absolving from the sins committed after Baptism?

A. I know that the priest has the power of absoiving from the sins committed after Baptism, because Jesus Christ granted that power to the priests of His Church when He said: "Receive ye the Holy Ghost. Whose sins you shall forgive, they are forgiven them; whose sins you shall retain, they are retained."

190. Q. How do the priests of the Church exercise the power of forgiving sins?

A. The priests of the Church exercise the power of forgiving sins by hearing the confession of sins, and granting pardon for them as ministers of God and in His Name.

191. Q. What must we do to receive the Sacrament of Penance worthily?

A. To receive the Sacrament of Penance worthily we must do five things:

1. We must examine our conscience.
2. We must have sorrow for our sins.
3. We must make a firm resolution never more to offend God.
4. We must confess our sins to the priest.
5. We must accept the penance which the priest gives us.

192. Q. What is the examination of conscience?

A. The examination of conscience is an earnest effort to recall to mind all the sins we have committed since our last worthy confession.

193. Q. How can we make a good examination of conscience?

A. We can make a good examination of conscience by calling to memory the Commandments of God, the precepts of the Church, the seven capital sins, and the particular duties of our state in life, to find out the sins we have committed.

194. Q. What should we do before beginning the examination of conscience?

A. Before beginning the examination of conscience we should pray to God to give us light to know our sins and grace to detest them.

LESSON EIGHTEENTH

On Contrition

En-deav′or (ĕn-dĕv′ẽr), to try hard.
Ex-cit′ed (ĕk-sīt′ĕd), increased, stirred up.
Fixed re-solve′ (rē-zŏlv′), deciding once for all.
Im-per′fect (ĭm-pẽr′fĕkt), good, but not the best.
Mere′ly nat′u-ral (mēr′lĭ năt′ū-răl), not caused by God's grace.
Mo′tives (mō′tĭvz), reasons.
Of-fend′ed (ō-fĕnd′ĕd), greatly displeased.
Pre-serv′er (prē-zûr′vĕr), the One who keeps us alive.
Prompt′ed (prŏmpt′ĕd), started.
Sov′er-eign (sŭv′ẽr-ĭn), above and greater than for any other misfortune.
U′ni-ver′sal (ū′nĭ-vûr′săl), taking in all, leaving out nothing.

195. Q. What is contrition, or sorrow for sin?

A. Contrition, or sorrow for sin, is a hatred of sin and a true grief of the soul for having offended God, with a firm purpose of sinning no more.

196. Q. What kind of sorrow should we have for our sins?

A. The sorrow we should have for our sins should be interior, supernatural, universal, and sovereign.

197. Q. What do you mean by saying that our sorrow should be interior?

A. When I say that our sorrow should be interior, I mean that it should come from the heart, and not merely from the lips.

198. Q. What do you mean by saying that our sorrow should be supernatural?

A. When I say that our sorrow should be supernatural, I mean that it should be prompted by the grace of God, and excited by motives which spring from faith, and not by merely natural motives.

199. Q. What do you mean by saying that our sorrow should be universal?

A. When I say that our sorrow should be universal, I mean that we should be sorry for all our mortal sins without exception.

200. Q. What do you mean when you say that our sorrow should be sovereign?

A. When I say that our sorrow should be sovereign, I mean that we should grieve more for having offended God than for any other evil that can befall us.

201. Q. Why should we be sorry for our sins?

A. We should be sorry for our sins, because sin is the greatest of evils and an offense against God our Creator, Preserver, and Redeemer, and because it shuts us out of Heaven and condemns us to the eternal pains of Hell.

202. Q. How many kinds of contrition are there?

A. There are two kinds of contrition: perfect contrition and imperfect contrition.

203. Q. What is perfect contrition?

A. Perfect contrition is that which fills us with sorrow and hatred for sin, because it offends God, who is infinitely good in Himself and worthy of all love.

204. Q. What is imperfect contrition?

A. Imperfect contrition is that by which we hate what offends God, because by it we lose Heaven and deserve Hell; or because sin is so hateful in itself.

205. Q. Is imperfect contrition sufficient for a worthy Confession?

A. Imperfect contrition is sufficient for a worthy Confession, but we should endeavor to have perfect contrition.

206. Q. What do you mean by a firm purpose of sinning no more?

A. By a firm purpose of sinning no more I mean a fixed resolve not only to avoid all mortal sin, but also its near occasions.

207. Q. What do you mean by the near occasions of sin?

A. By the near occasions of sin I mean all the persons, places, and things that may easily lead us into sin.

LESSON NINETEENTH

On Confession

Ac-cuse′ (ă-kūz′), to charge with having committed a fault.

Ad-mon′ish (ăd-mŏn′ĭsh), to kindly warn of faults.

Alms′giv-ing (ämz′gĭv-ĭng), helping the poor.

Cir′cum-stanc-es (sûr′kŭm-stăn-sĕz), facts that explain the thing better.

Con-ceal′ (kŏn-sēl′), to hide or keep back.

Cor′po-ral (kôr′pō-răl), helping the body.

Coun′sel (koun′sĕl), to advise.

Du′ly au′thor-ized (dū′lĭ ŏ′thŏr-īzd), appointed by the Bishop.

Ex-ag′ger-at′ing ĕg-zăj′ĕr-āt′-ĭng), making things worse than they are.

Har′bor (här′bĕr), to give shelter to.

Har′bor-less (här′bĕr-lĕs), persons without a home.

Ills, sufferings and misfortunes.

Pa′tient (pā′shĕnt), without complaining.

Ran′som (răn′sŭm), to buy freedom for a slave or prisoner.

Re-peat′ (rē-pēt′), to say or do over again.

Sat′is-fac′tion (săt′ĭs-făk′shŭn), reparation or making up for the injury done.

Spir′it-u-al (spĭr′ĭ-tū-ăl), helping the soul.

Tem′po-ral (tĕm′pō-răl), lasting for a time only.

Worth′less (wûrth′lĕs), no good at all.

208. Q. What is Confession?

A. Confession is the telling of our sins to a duly authorized priest, for the purpose of obtaining forgiveness.

209. Q. What sins are we bound to confess?

A. We are bound to confess all our mortal sins, but it is well also to confess our venial sins.

210. Q. Which are the chief qualities of a good Confession?

A. The chief qualities of a good Confession are three: it must be humble, sincere, and entire.

211. Q. When is our Confession humble?

A. Our Confession is humble, when we accuse ourselves of our sins, with a deep sense of shame and sorrow for having offended God.

212. Q. When is our Confession sincere?

A. Our Confession is sincere, when we tell our sins honestly and truthfully, neither exaggerating nor excusing them.

213. Q. When is our Confession entire?

A. Our Confession is entire, when we tell the number and kinds of our sins and the circumstances which change their nature.

214. Q. What should we do if we cannot remember the number of our sins?

A. If we cannot remember the number of our sins, we should tell the number as nearly as possible, and say how often we may have sinned in a day, a week, or a month, and how long the habit or practice has lasted.

215. Q. Is our Confession worthy if, without our fault, we forget to confess a mortal sin?

A. If without our fault we forget to confess a mortal sin, our Confession is worthy, and the sin is forgiven; but it must be told in Confession if it again comes to our mind.

216. Q. Is it a grievous offense willfully to conceal a mortal sin in Confession?

A. It is a grievous offense willfully to conceal a mortal sin in Confession, because we thereby tell a lie to the Holy Ghost, and make our Confession worthless.

217. Q. What must he do who has willfully concealed a mortal sin in Confession?

A. He who has willfully concealed a mortal sin in Confession must not only confess it, but must also repeat all the sins he has committed since his last worthy Confession.

218. Q. Why does the priest give us a penance after Confession?

A. The priest gives us a penance after Confession, that we may satisfy God for the temporal punishment due to our sins.

219. Q. Does not the Sacrament of Penance remit all punishment due to sin?

A. The Sacrament of Penance remits the eternal punishment due to sin, but it does not always remit the temporal punishment which God requires as satisfaction for our sins.

220. Q. Why does God require a temporal punishment as a satisfaction for sin?

A. God requires a temporal punishment as a satisfaction for sin, to teach us the great evil of sin and to prevent us from falling again.

221. Q. Which are the chief means by which we satisfy God for the temporal punishment due to sin?

A. The chief means by which we satisfy God for the temporal punishment due to sin are: Prayer, Fasting, Almsgiving, all spiritual and corporal works of mercy, and the patient suffering of the ills of life.

222. Q. Which are the chief spiritual works of mercy?

A. The chief spiritual works of mercy are seven: To admonish the sinner, to instruct the ignorant, to counsel the doubtful, to comfort the sorrowful, to bear wrongs patiently, to forgive all injuries, and to pray for the living and the dead.

223. Q. Which are the chief corporal works of mercy?

A. The chief corporal works of mercy are seven: To feed the hungry, to give drink to the thirsty, to clothe the naked, to ransom the captive, to harbor the harborless, to visit the sick, and to bury the dead.

LESSON TWENTIETH

On the Manner of Making a Good Confession

Con-fes′sion-al (kŏn-fĕsh′ŭn-ăl), the box or stall in which the priest hears Confessions.

Con-fes′sor (kŏn-fĕs′ĕr), the priest hearing Confessions.

Re-new′ (rē-nū′), say or repeat.

224. Q. What should we do on entering the confessional?

A. On entering the confessional we should kneel, make the Sign of the Cross, and say to the priest, "Bless me, Father"; then add, "I confess to Almighty God and to you, Father, that I have sinned."

225. Q. Which are the first things we should tell the priest in Confession?

A. The first things we should tell the priest in Confession are the time of our last Confession, and whether we said the penance and went to Holy Communion.

226. Q. After telling the time of our last Confession and Communion what should we do?

A. After telling the time of our last Confession and Communion we should confess all the mortal sins we have since committed, and all the venial sins we may wish to mention.

227. Q. What must we do when the confessor asks us questions?

A. When the confessor asks us questions we must answer them truthfully and clearly.

228. Q. What should we do after telling our sins?

A. After telling our sins we should listen with attention to the advice which the confessor may think proper to give.

229. Q. How should we end our Confession?

A. We should end our Confession by saying, "I also accuse myself of all the sins of my past life," telling, if we choose, one or several of our past sins.

230. Q. What should we do while the priest is giving us absolution?

A. While the priest is giving us absolution we should from our heart renew the Act of Contrition.

LESSON TWENTY-FIRST

On Indulgences

Ap-ply′ing (ăp-plī′ĭng), giving the benefit of.
En-joined′ (ĕn-joind′), ordered to be done.
Li′cense (lī′sĕns), permission to do something.
Par′tial (pär′shăl), in part only.
Ple′na-ry (plē′nȧ-rĭ), full, complete.
Re-mis′sion (rē-mĭsh′ŭn), taking away.
Su′per-a-bun′dant (sū′pĕr-ȧ-bŭn′-dănt), more than was necessary.
Treas′ur-y (trĕszh′ūr-ĭ) a place for storing riches.

231. Q. What is an Indulgence?
A. An Indulgence is the remission in whole or in part of the temporal punishment due to sin.

232. Q. Is an Indulgence a pardon of sin, or a license to commit sin?
A. An Indulgence is not a pardon of sin, nor a license to commit sin, and one who is in a state of mortal sin cannot gain an Indulgence.

233. Q. How many kinds of Indulgences are there?
A. There are two kinds of Indulgences—Plenary and Partial.

234. Q. What is a Plenary Indulgence?
A. A Plenary Indulgence is the full remission of the temporal punishment due to sin.

235. Q. What is a Partial Indulgence?

A. A Partial Indulgence is the remission of a part of the temporal punishment due to sin.

236. Q. How does the Church by means of Indulgences remit the temporal punishment due to sin?

A. The Church by means of Indulgences remits the temporal punishment due to sin by applying to us the merits of Jesus Christ, and the superabundant satisfactions of the Blessed Virgin Mary and of the Saints; which merits and satisfactions are its spiritual treasury.

237. Q. What must we do to gain an Indulgence?

A. To gain an Indulgence we must be in the state of grace and perform the works enjoined.

LESSON TWENTY-SECOND

On the Holy Eucharist

Com-mem´o-ra´tion (kŏ-mĕm´ō-rā´shŭn), a calling to mind.

Con´se-cra´tion (kŏn´sĕ-krā´shŭn), the act of changing the bread and wine into the sacred Body and Blood of Christ.

Di-vin´i-ty (dĭ-vĭn´ĭ-tĭ), the nature of God.

Min´is-try (mĭn´ĭs-trĭ), by means of.

Sen´ses (sĕn´sĕz), the sight, the taste, the touch.

Tran´sub-stan´ti-a´tion (trăn´sŭb-stăn´shē-ā´shŭn), the change of one thing into another without any change in its appearance.

238. Q. What is the Holy Eucharist?

A. The Holy Eucharist is the Sacrament which contains the Body and Blood, Soul and Divinity, of Our Lord Jesus Christ under the appearances of bread and wine.

239. Q. When did Christ institute the Holy Eucharist?

A. Christ instituted the Holy Eucharist at the Last Supper, the night before He died.

240. Q. Who were present when Our Lord instituted the Holy Eucharist?

A. When Our Lord instituted the Holy Eucharist the twelve Apostles were present.

241. Q. How did Our Lord institute the Holy Eucharist?

A. Our Lord instituted the Holy Eucharist by taking bread, blessing, breaking, and giving to His Apostles, saying: "Take ye and eat, This is My Body"; and then by taking the cup of wine, blessing and giving it, saying to them: "Drink ye all of this. This is My Blood which shall be shed for the remission of sins. Do this for a commemoration of Me."

242. Q. What happened when Our Lord said, "This is My Body; this is My Blood?"

A. When Our Lord said, "This is My Body," the substance of the bread was changed into the substance of His Body; when He said, "This is My Blood," the substance of the wine was changed into the substance of His Blood.

243. Q. Is Jesus Christ whole and entire both under the form of bread and under the form of wine?

A. Jesus Christ is whole and entire both under the form of bread and under the form of wine.

244. Q. Did anything remain of the bread and wine after their substance had been changed into the substance of the Body and Blood of Our Lord?

A. After the substance of the bread and wine had been changed into the substance of the Body and Blood of Our Lord there remained only the appearances of bread and wine.

245. Q. What do you mean by the appearances of bread and wine?

A. By the appearances of bread and wine I mean the figure, the color, the taste, and whatever appears to the senses.

246. Q. What is this change of the bread and wine into the Body and Blood of Our Lord called?

A. This change of the bread and wine into the Body and Blood of Our Lord is called Transubstantiation.

247. Q. How was the substance of the bread and wine changed into the substance of the Body and Blood of Christ?

A. The substance of the bread and wine was changed into the substance of the Body and Blood of Christ by His almighty power.

248. Q. Does this change of bread and wine into the Body and Blood of Christ continue to be made in the Church?

A. This change of bread and wine into the Body and Blood of Christ continues to be made in the Church by Jesus Christ through the ministry of His priests.

249. Q. When did Christ give His priests the power to change bread and wine into His Body and Blood?

A. Christ gave His priests the power to change bread and wine into His Body and Blood when He said to the Apostles, "Do this in commemoration of Me."

250. Q. How do the priests exercise this power of changing bread and wine into the Body and Blood of Christ?

A. The priests exercise this power of changing bread and wine into the Body and Blood of Christ through the words of Consecration in the Mass, which are the words of Christ: "This is My Body; this is My Blood."

LESSON TWENTY-THIRD

On the Ends for Which the Holy Eucharist Was Instituted

Ab-stain′ing (ăb-stān′ĭng), keeping from.

A-dor′ing (ȧ-dōr′ĭng), saying to God that He is all and we are nothing.

Au′thor (ô′thĕr), He from whom a thing comes.

In′cli-na′tions (ĭn′klĭ-nā′shŭnz), strong likings.

Live′ly (līv′lĭ), heartfelt, strong.

Nour′ish (nŭr′ĭsh), to support with food.

Pledge (plĕj), promise.

Sac′ri-fice (săk′rĭ-fīs), an offering made to God.

251. Q. Why did Christ institute the Holy Eucharist?

A. Christ instituted the Holy Eucharist:

1. To unite us to Himself and to nourish our soul with His divine life.
2. To increase sanctifying grace and all virtues in our soul.
3. To lessen our evil inclinations.
4. To be a pledge of everlasting life.
5. To fit our bodies for a glorious resurrection.
6. To continue the sacrifice of the Cross in His Church.

252. Q. How are we united to Jesus Christ in the Holy Eucharist?

A. We are united to Jesus Christ in the Holy Eucharist by means of Holy Communion.

253. Q. What is Holy Communion?

A. Holy Communion is the receiving of the Body and Blood of Christ.

254. Q. What is necessary to make a good Communion?

A. To make a good Communion it is necessary to be in the state of sanctifying grace, to have a right intention, and to obey the laws of fasting. (See Q. 257.)

255. Q. Does he who receives Communion in mortal sin receive the Body and Blood of Christ?

A. He who receives Communion in mortal sin receives the Body and Blood of Christ, but does not receive His grace, and he commits a great sacrilege.

256. Q. Is it enough to be free from mortal sin to receive plentifully the graces of Holy Communion?

A. To receive plentifully the graces of Holy Communion it is not enough to be free from mortal sin, but we should be free from all affection to venial sin, and should make acts of faith, hope, and love.

257. Q. What is the fast necessary for Holy Communion?

A. The fast necessary for Holy Communion is to abstain from all food, beverages, and alcoholic drinks for one hour before Holy Communion. Water may be taken at any time. The sick may take food, non-alcoholic drinks, and any medicine up to Communion time.[1]

258. Q. Is any one ever allowed to receive Holy Communion when not fasting?

A. Any one in danger of death is allowed to receive Holy Communion when not fasting or when it is necessary to save the Blessed Sacrament from insult or injury.

1. This answer has been changed in the 1977 printing to bring it up to date with the current rules.

259. Q. When are we bound to receive Holy Communion?

A. We are bound to receive Holy Communion, under pain of mortal sin, during the Easter time and when in danger of death.

260. Q. Is it well to receive Holy Communion often?

A. It is well to receive Holy Communion often, as nothing is a greater aid to a holy life than often to receive the Author of all grace and the Source of all good.

261. Q. What should we do after Holy Communion?

A. After Holy Communion we should spend some time in adoring Our Lord, in thanking Him for the grace we have received, and in asking Him for the blessings we need.

LESSON TWENTY-FOURTH

On the Sacrifice of the Mass

Ack-nowl′edge (ăk-nŏl′ĕj), to show that we believe.

Con-sum′ing (kŏn-sūm′ĭng), destroying by receiving as food and drink.

Med′i-tate (mĕd′ĭ-tāt), to think over in our mind.

Re′al-ly (rē′ăl-lĭ) truly, and not in appearance only.

Rec′o-llec′tion (rĕk′ŏ-lĕk′shŭn), remembering where we are.

262. Q. When and where are the bread and wine changed into the Body and Blood of Christ?

A. The bread and wine are changed into the Body and Blood of Christ at the Consecration in the Mass.

263. Q. What is the Mass?

A. The Mass is the unbloody Sacrifice of the Body and Blood of Christ.

264. Q. What is a sacrifice?

A. A sacrifice is the offering of an object by a priest to God alone, and the consuming of it to acknowledge that He is the Creator and Lord of all things.

265. Q. Is the Mass the same Sacrifice as that of the Cross?

A. The Mass is the same Sacrifice as that of the Cross.

266. Q. How is the Mass the same Sacrifice as that of the Cross?

A. The Mass is the same sacrifice as that of the Cross because the offering and the priest are the same—Christ our Blessed Lord; and the ends for which the Sacrifice of the Mass is offered are the same as those of the Sacrifice of the Cross.

267. Q. What were the ends for which the Sacrifice of the Cross was offered?

A. The ends for which the Sacrifice of the Cross was offered were: 1) To honor and glorify God; 2) To thank Him for all the graces bestowed on the whole world; 3) To satisfy God's justice for the sins of men; 4) To obtain all graces and blessings.

268. Q. Is there any difference between the Sacrifice of the Cross and the Sacrifice of the Mass?

A. Yes; the manner in which the Sacrifice is offered is different. On the Cross Christ really shed His blood and was really slain; in the Mass there is no real shedding of blood nor real death, because Christ can die no more; but the Sacrifice of the Mass, through the separate consecration of the bread and the wine, represents His death on the Cross.

269. Q. How should we assist at Mass?

A. We should assist at Mass with great interior recollection and piety and with every outward mark of respect and devotion.

270. Q. Which is the best manner of hearing Mass?

A. The best manner of hearing Mass is to offer it to God with the priest for the same purpose for which it is said, to meditate on Christ's sufferings and death, and to go to Holy Communion.

LESSON TWENTY-FIFTH

On Extreme Unction and Holy Orders

Con-fer′ (kŏn-fĕr′), to give, bestow.
Dis-pen′sers (dĭs-pĕn′sĕrz), those who give out.
Ex-treme′ (ĕks-trēm′), the very last.
Res′ig-na′tion (rĕz′ĭg-nā′shŭn), accepting God's Will.
Re-store′ (rē-stôr′), bring back.
Re-sult′ (rē-zŭlt′), what comes of a thing.
Unc′tion (ŭnk′shŭn), rubbing with oil.

271. Q. What is the Sacrament of Extreme Unction?

A. Extreme Unction is the Sacrament which, through the anointing and prayer of the priest, gives health and strength to the soul, and sometimes to the body, when we are in danger of death from sickness.

272. Q. When should we receive Extreme Unction?

A. We should receive Extreme Unction when we are in danger of death from sickness, or from a wound or accident.

273. Q. Should we wait until we are in extreme danger before we receive Extreme Unction?

A. We should not wait until we are in extreme danger before we receive Extreme Unction, but if possible we should receive it whilst we have the use of our senses.

274. Q. Which are the effects of the Sacrament of Extreme Unction?

A. The effects of Extreme Unction are: 1) To comfort us in the pains of sickness and to strengthen us against temptation; 2) To remit venial sins and to cleanse our soul from the remains of sin; 3) To restore us to health, when God sees fit.

275. Q. What do you mean by the remains of sin?

A. By the remains of sin I mean the inclination to evil and the weakness of the will which are the result of our sins, and which remain after our sins have been forgiven.

276. Q. How should we receive the Sacrament of Extreme Unction?

A. We should receive the Sacrament of Extreme Unction in the state of grace, and with lively faith and resignation to the Will of God.

277. Q. Who is the minister of the Sacrament of Extreme Unction?

A. The priest is the minister of the Sacrament of Extreme Unction.

278. Q. What is the Sacrament of Holy Orders?

A. Holy Orders is a Sacrament by which bishops, priests, and other ministers of the Church are ordained and receive the power and grace to perform their sacred duties.

279. Q. What is necessary to receive Holy Orders worthily?

A. To receive Holy Orders worthily it is necessary to be in the state of grace, to have the necessary knowledge and a divine call to this sacred office.

280. Q. How should Christians look upon the priests of the Church?

A. Christians should look upon the priests of the Church as the messengers of God and the dispensers of His mysteries.

281. Q. Who can confer the Sacrament of Holy Orders?

A. Bishops can confer the Sacrament of Holy Orders.

LESSON TWENTY-SIXTH

On Matrimony

Bond (bŏnd), tie, union.
Civ′il (sĭv′ĭl) **effects**, what concerns public order.
Com-ply′ (kŏm-plī′) **with**, to act according to, obey.
Con′tract (kŏn′trăkt), a binding agreement.
Dig′ni-ty (dĭg′nĭ-tĭ), high rank.
Dis-solved′ (dĭ-zŏlvd′), broken up.
Ed′u-ca′tion (ĕd′ū-kā′shŭn), training of mind and heart.
Has′ti-ly (hās′tĭ-lĭ), without thinking well beforehand.
Hu′man (hū′măn), belonging to man.
In-dif′fer-ence (ĭn-dĭf′ĕr-ĕns), caring little or nothing about God and religion.
In-ten′tion (ĭn-tĕn′shŭn), motive.
Law′ful (lô′fŭl), according to law.
Mo′tives (mō′tĭvz), reasons.
Weak′ness-es (wēk′nĕs-ĕz), faults and failings.

282. Q. What is the Sacrament of Matrimony?

A. The Sacrament of Matrimony is the Sacrament which unites a Christian man and woman in lawful marriage.

283. Q. Can a Christian man and woman be united in lawful marriage in any other way than by the Sacrament of Matrimony?

A. A Christian man and woman cannot be united in lawful marriage in any other way than by the Sacrament of Matrimony, because Christ raised marriage to the dignity of a Sacrament.

284. Q. Can the bond of Christian marriage be dissolved by any human power?

A. The bond of Christian marriage cannot be dissolved by any human power.

285. Q. Which are the effects of the Sacrament of Matrimony?

A. The effects of the Sacrament of Matrimony are: 1) To sanctify the love of husband and wife; 2) To give them grace to bear with each other's weaknesses; 3) To enable them to bring up their children in the fear and love of God.

286. Q. To receive the Sacrament of Matrimony worthily is it necessary to be in the state of grace?

A. To receive the Sacrament of Matrimony worthily it is necessary to be in the state of grace, and it is necessary also to comply with the laws of the Church.

287. Q. Who has the right to make laws concerning the Sacrament of marriage?

A. The Church alone has the right to make laws concerning the Sacrament of marriage, though the state also has the right to make laws concerning the civil effects of the marriage contract.

288. Q. Does the Church forbid the marriage of Catholics with persons who have a different religion or no religion at all?

A. The Church does forbid the marriage of Catholics with persons who have a different religion or no religion at all.

289. Q. Why does the Church forbid the marriage of Catholics with persons who have a different religion or no religion at all?

A. The Church forbids the marriage of Catholics with persons who have a different religion or no religion at all, because such marriages generally lead to indifference, loss of faith, and to the neglect of the religious education of the children.

290. Q. Why do many marriages prove unhappy?

A. Many marriages prove unhappy because they are entered into hastily and without worthy motives.

291. Q. How should Christians prepare for a holy and happy marriage?

A. Christians should prepare for a holy and happy marriage by receiving the Sacraments of Penance and Holy Eucharist; by begging God to grant them a pure intention and to direct their choice; and by seeking the advice of their parents and the blessing of their pastors.

LESSON TWENTY-SEVENTH

On the Sacramentals

Dis′po-si′tions (dĭs′pō-zĭsh′-ŭnz), feelings, state of mind.
Ex-pres′ses (ĕks-prĕs′ĕz), shows by words and actions.
Fre′quent (frē′kwĕnt), happening often.
Ob′sta-cle (ŏb′stȧ-k'l), that which hinders.
Powers of Darkness, the devil and his bad angels.
Sac′ra-men′tals (săk′rȧ-mĕn′-tălz), something blessed or set apart by the Church.
Sol′emn (sŏl′ĕm), with special ceremonies.

292. Q. What is a sacramental?

A. A sacramental is anything set apart or blessed by the Church to excite good thoughts and to increase devotion, and through these movements of the heart to remit venial sin.

293. Q. What is the difference between the Sacraments and the sacramentals?

A. The difference between the Sacraments and the sacramentals is: 1) The Sacraments were instituted by Jesus Christ and the sacramentals were instituted by the Church; 2) The Sacraments give grace of themselves when we place no obstacle in the way; the sacramentals excite in us pious dispositions, by means of which we may obtain grace.

294. Q. Which is the chief sacramental used in the Church?

A. The chief sacramental used in the Church is the Sign of the Cross.

295. Q. How do we make the Sign of the Cross?

A. We make the Sign of the Cross by putting the right hand to the forehead, then on the breast, and then to the left and right shoulders, saying, "In the name of the Father and of the Son, and of the Holy Ghost. Amen."

296. Q. Why do we make the Sign of the Cross?

A. We make the Sign of the Cross to show that we are Christians and to profess our belief in the chief mysteries of our religion.

297. Q. How is the Sign of the Cross a profession of faith in the chief mysteries of our religion?

A. The Sign of the Cross is a profession of faith in the chief mysteries of our religion because it expresses the mysteries of the Unity and Trinity of God and of the Incarnation and death of Our Lord.

298. Q. How does the Sign of the Cross express the mystery of the Unity and Trinity of God?

A. The words, "In the name," express the Unity of God; the words that follow, "of the Father, and of the Son, and of the Holy Ghost," express the mystery of the Trinity.

299. Q. How does the Sign of the Cross express the mystery of the Incarnation and death of Our Lord?

A. The Sign of the Cross expresses the mystery of the Incarnation by reminding us that the Son of God, having become man, suffered death on the Cross.

300. Q. What other sacramental is in very frequent use?

A. Another sacramental in very frequent use is holy water.

301. Q. What is holy water?

A. Holy water is water blessed by the priest with solemn prayer to beg God's blessing on those who use it, and protection from the powers of darkness.

302. Q. Are there other sacramentals besides the Sign of the Cross and holy water?

A. Besides the Sign of the Cross and holy water there are many other sacramentals, such as blessed candles, ashes, palms, crucifixes, images of the Blessed Virgin and of the Saints, rosaries, and scapulars.

LESSON TWENTY-EIGHTH

On Prayer

Af-flic′tions (ă-flĭk′shŭnz), sufferings in mind or body.

At-ten′tion (ă-tĕn′shŭn), thinking of what you are saying.

A-vail′ (ȧ-vāl′), profit or advantage.

Con-fi′te-or (kŏn-fē′tā-ōr), I confess.

De-pend′ence (dē-pĕn′dĕns), looking to Him for support.

Dis-trac′tions (dĭs-trăk′shŭnz), thinking of other things besides your prayers.

Help′less-ness (hĕlp′lĕs-nĕs), weakness, like a child's.

303. Q. Is there any other means of obtaining God's grace than the Sacraments?

A. There is another means of obtaining God's grace, and it is prayer.

304. Q. What is prayer?

A. Prayer is the lifting up of our minds and hearts to God to adore Him, to thank Him for His benefits, to ask His forgiveness, and to beg of Him all the graces we need whether for soul or body.

305. Q. Is prayer necessary to salvation?

A. Prayer is necessary to salvation, and without it no one having the use of reason can be saved.

306. Q. At what particular times should we pray?

A. We should pray particularly on Sundays and holy days, every morning and night, in all dangers, temptations, and afflictions.

307. Q. How should we pray?

A. We should pray: 1) With attention; 2) With a sense of our own helplessness and dependence upon God; 3) With a great desire for the graces we beg of God; 4) With trust in God's goodness; 5) With perseverance.

308. Q. Which are the prayers most recommended to us?

A. The prayers most recommended to us are the *Lord's Prayer*, the *Hail Mary*, the *Apostles' Creed*, the *Confiteor*, and the *Acts of Faith*, *Hope*, *Love*, and *Contrition*.

309. Q. Are prayers said with distractions of any avail?

A. Prayers said with willful distractions are of no avail.

LESSON TWENTY-NINTH

On the Commandments of God

Bear false witness, to tell lies about.
Bond´age (bŏn´dȧj), slavery.
Con-firmed´ (kŏn-fûrmd´), renewed, gave them new force.
Cov´et (kŭv´ĕt), to be greedy for, to desire.
Goods, riches, or whatever he owns.
Grav´en (grāv´n), cut out of wood or stone.
Hon´or, to respect and obey.
In vain, without necessity or in fun.
Op-posed´ (ŏ-pōzd´), against.
Shun (shŭn), to avoid.
Strange, false.
Take, utter, invoke.

310. Q. Is it enough to belong to God's Church in order to be saved?

A. It is not enough to belong to the Church in order to be saved, but we must also keep the Commandments of God and of the Church.

311. Q. Which are the Commandments that contain the whole law of God?

A. The Commandments which contain the whole law of God are these two: 1) Thou shalt love the Lord thy God with thy whole heart, with thy whole soul, with thy whole strength, and with thy whole mind; 2) Thou shalt love thy neighbor as thyself.

312. Q. Why do these two Commandments of the love of God and of our neighbor contain the whole law of God?

A. These two Commandments of the love of God and of our neighbor contain the whole law of God because all the other Commandments are given either to help us to keep these two, or to direct us how to shun what is opposed to them.

313. Q. Which are the Commandments of God?

A. The Commandments of God are these ten:

1. I am the Lord thy God, who brought thee out of the land of Egypt, out of the house of bondage. Thou shalt not have strange gods before Me. Thou shalt not make to thyself a graven thing, nor the likeness of anything that is in heaven above, or in the earth beneath, nor of those things that are in the waters under the earth. Thou shalt not adore them, nor serve them.
2. Thou shalt not take the name of the Lord thy God in vain.
3. Remember thou keep holy the Sabbath day.
4. Honor thy father and thy mother.
5. Thou shalt not kill.
6. Thou shalt not commit adultery.
7. Thou shalt not steal.
8. Thou shalt not bear false witness against thy neighbor.
9. Thou shalt not covet thy neighbor's wife.
10. Thou shalt not covet thy neighbor's goods.

314. Q. Who gave the Ten Commandments?

A. God Himself gave the Ten Commandments to Moses on Mount Sinai, and Christ Our Lord confirmed them.

LESSON THIRTIETH

On the First Commandment

Ac-knowl′edge (ăk-nŏl′ĕj), to declare their belief in.

A-dore′ (ȧ-dōr′), to give God the honor due Him alone.

At-trib′ut-ing (ă-trĭb′ū-tĭng), referring.

Charms (chärmz), objects worn on the body and supposed to bring luck or drive away evil.

Con-fess′ (kŏn-fĕs′), declare their faith in.

Ex′pec-ta′tion (ĕks′pĕk-tā′shŭn), a looking forward to.

Her′e-tics (hĕr′ĕ-tĭks), baptized persons not Catholics.

In′fi-dels (ĭn′fĭ-dĕlz), persons never baptized.

Me′di-ums (mē′dĭ-ŭmz), people who claim that through them the living can talk to the dead.

Pre-sump′tion (prē-zŭmp′shŭn), taking for granted the saving of one's soul.

Rash (răsh), foolish.

Spells (spĕlz), certain words, the saying of which is supposed to possess magical power.

Spir′it-ists (spĭr′ĭ-tĭsts), people who believe that the living can talk with the dead.

Wor′ship (wûr′shĭp), religious service.

315. Q. What is the first Commandment?

A. The first Commandment is: "I am the Lord thy God: thou shalt not have strange gods before Me."

316. Q. How does the first Commandment help us to keep the great Commandment of the love of God?

A. The first Commandment helps us to keep the great Commandment of the love of God because it commands us to adore God alone.

317. Q. How do we adore God?

A. We adore God by faith, hope, and charity, by prayer and sacrifice.

318. Q. How may the first Commandment be broken?

A. The first Commandment may be broken by giving to a creature the honor which belongs to God alone; by false worship; and by attributing to a creature a perfection which belongs to God alone.

319. Q. Do those who make use of spells and charms, or who believe in dreams, in mediums, spiritists, fortune-tellers, and the like, sin against the first Commandment?

A. Those who make use of spells and charms, or who believe in dreams, in mediums, spiritists, fortune-tellers and the like, sin against the first Commandment, because they attribute to creatures perfections which belong to God alone.

320. Q. Are sins against faith, hope, and charity also sins against the first Commandment?

A. Sins against faith, hope, and charity are also sins against the first Commandment.

321. Q. How does a person sin against faith?

A. A person sins against faith: 1) by not trying to know what God has taught; 2) by refusing to believe all that God has taught; 3) by neglecting to profess his belief in what God has taught.

322. Q. **How do we fail to try to know what God has taught?**

A. We fail to try to know what God has taught by neglecting to learn the Christian doctrine.

323. Q. **Who are they who do not believe all that God has taught?**

A. They who do not believe all that God has taught are the heretics and infidels.

324. Q. **Who are they who neglect to profess their belief in what God has taught?**

A. They who neglect to profess their belief in what God has taught are all those who fail to acknowledge the true Church in which they really believe.

325. Q. **Can they who fail to profess their faith in the true Church in which they believe expect to be saved while in that state?**

A. They who fail to profess their faith in the true Church in which they believe cannot expect to be saved while in that state, for Christ has said: "Whoever shall deny Me before men, I will also deny him before My Father who is in Heaven."

326. Q. **Are we obliged to make open profession of our faith?**

A. We are obliged to make open profession of our faith as often as God's honor, our neighbor's spiritual good, or our own requires it. "Whosoever," says Christ, "shall confess Me before men, I will also confess him before My Father who is in heaven."

327. Q. **Which are the sins against hope?**

A. The sins against hope are presumption and despair.

328. Q. What is presumption?

A. Presumption is a rash expectation of salvation without making proper use of the necessary means to obtain it.

329. Q. What is despair?

A. Despair is the loss of hope in God's mercy.

330. Q. How do we sin against the love of God?

A. We sin against the love of God by all sin, but particularly by mortal sin.

LESSON THIRTY-FIRST

The First Commandment—On the Honor and Invocation of Saints

Ap-proves′ (ă-prōōvz′), is in accord with.
Breth′ren (brĕth′rĕn), belonging to the one family.
De-rived′ (dē-rīvd′), resulting from.
En-liv′en (ĕn-līv′n), to stir up.
Im′i-tate (ĭm′ĭ-tāt), to copy.
In′ter-cess′ion (ĭn′tĕr-sĕsh′ŭn), pleading.
In′vo-ca′tion (ĭn′vō-kā′shŭn), calling upon.
Me-mo′ri-als (mĕ-mō′rĭ-ălz), something to remind us.
Rel′ics (rĕl′ĭks), bones of the saints or objects connected with them or Our Lord.
Rep′re-sen-ta′tions (rĕp′rĕ-zĕn-tā′-shŭnz), means of showing the appearance of absent ones.

331. Q. Does the first Commandment forbid the honoring of the Saints?

A. The first Commandment does not forbid the honoring of the Saints, but rather approves of it; because by honoring the Saints, who are the chosen friends of God, we honor God Himself.

332. Q. Does the first Commandment forbid us to pray to the Saints?

A. The first Commandment does not forbid us to pray to the Saints.

333. Q. What do we mean by praying to the Saints?

A. By praying to the Saints we mean the asking of their help and prayers.

334. Q. How do we know that the Saints hear us?

A. We know that the Saints hear us, because they are with God, who makes our prayers known to them.

335. Q. Why do we believe that the Saints will help us?

A. We believe that the Saints will help us because both they and we are members of the same Church, and they love us as their brethren.

336. Q. How are the Saints and we members of the same Church?

A. The Saints and we are members of the same Church, because the Church in Heaven and the Church on earth are one and the same Church, and all its members are in communion with one another.

337. Q. What is the communion of the members of the Church called?

A. The communion of the members of the Church is called the communion of saints.

338. Q. What does the communion of saints mean?

A. The communion of saints means the union which exists between the members of the Church on earth with one another, and with the blessed in Heaven and with the suffering souls in Purgatory.

339. Q. What benefits are derived from the communion of saints?

A. The following benefits are derived from the communion of saints—the faithful on earth assist one another by their prayers and good works, and they are aided by the intercession of the Saints in Heaven, while both the Saints in Heaven and the faithful on earth help the souls in Purgatory.

340. Q. Does the first Commandment forbid us to honor relics?

A. The first Commandment does not forbid us to honor relics, because relics are the bodies of the Saints, or objects directly connected with them or with Our Lord.

341. Q. Does the first Commandment forbid the making of images?

A. The first Commandment does forbid the making of images if they are made to be adored as gods, but it does not forbid the making of them to put us in mind of Jesus Christ, His Blessed Mother, and the Saints.

342. Q. Is it right to show respect to the pictures and images of Christ and His Saints?

A. It is right to show respect to the pictures and images of Christ and His Saints, because they are the representations and memorials of them.

343. Q. Is it allowed to pray to the crucifix or to the images and relics of the Saints?

A. It is not allowed to pray to the crucifix or images and relics of the Saints, for they have no life, nor power to help us, nor sense to hear us.

344. Q. Why do we pray before the crucifix and the images and relics of the Saints?

A. We pray before the crucifix and images and relics of the Saints because they enliven our devotion by exciting pious affections and desires, and by reminding us of Christ and of the Saints, that we may imitate their virtues.

LESSON THIRTY-SECOND

From the Second to the Fourth Commandment

Blas′phe-my (blȧs′fĕ-mĭ), saying or doing something disrespectful to God or holy things.

Curs′ing (kûrs′ĭng), calling upon God to bring evils on another.

De-lib′er-ate (dē-lĭb′ĕr-ât), well considered beforehand.

Due (dū), right and proper.

Law′ful au-thor′i-ty (lô′fŭl ô-thŏr′ĭ-tĭ), one having the right to command.

Ob-serv′ance (ŏb-zûr′văns), keeping holy.

Old Law, the law made for the Jews until Christ came.

Pro-fane′ (prō-fān′), wicked or irreverent.

Rev′er-ence (rĕv′ĕr-ĕns), great respect.

Sab′bath (săb′ȧth), seventh day of week.

Ser′vile (sûr′vĭl), performed with bodily labor.

345. Q. What is the second Commandment?

A. The second Commandment is: "Thou shalt not take the name of the Lord thy God in vain."

346. Q. What are we commanded by the second Commandment?

A. We are commanded by the second Commandment to speak with reverence of God and of the Saints, and of all holy things, and to keep our lawful oaths and vows.

347. Q. What is an oath?

A. An oath is the calling upon God to witness the truth of what we say.

348. Q. When may we take an oath?

A. We may take an oath when it is ordered by lawful authority or required for God's honor or for our own or our neighbor's good.

349. Q. What is necessary to make an oath lawful?

A. To make an oath lawful it is necessary that what we swear to, be true, and that there be a sufficient cause for taking an oath.

350. Q. What is a vow?

A. A vow is a deliberate promise made to God to do something that is pleasing to Him.

351. Q. Is it a sin not to fulfill our vows?

A. Not to fulfill our vows is a sin, mortal or venial, according to the nature of the vow and the intention we had in making it.

352. Q. What is forbidden by the second Commandment?

A. The second Commandment forbids all false, rash, unjust, and unnecessary oaths, blasphemy, cursing, and profane words.

353. Q. What is the third Commandment?

A. The third Commandment is: "Remember thou keep holy the Sabbath day."

354. Q. What are we commanded by the third Commandment?

A. By the third Commandment we are commanded to keep holy the Lord's day and the Holy Days of Obligation, on which we are to give our time to the service and worship of God.

355. Q. How are we to worship God on Sundays and Holy Days of Obligation?

A. We are to worship God on Sundays and Holy Days of Obligation by hearing Mass, by prayer, and by other good works.

356. Q. Are the Sabbath day and the Sunday the same?

A. The Sabbath day and the Sunday are not the same. The Sabbath is the seventh day of the week, and is the day which was kept holy in the Old Law; the Sunday is the first day of the week, and is the day which is kept holy in the New Law.

357. Q. Why does the Church command us to keep the Sunday holy instead of the Sabbath?

A. The Church commands us to keep the Sunday holy instead of the Sabbath because on Sunday Christ rose from the dead, and on Sunday He sent the Holy Ghost upon the Apostles.

358. Q. What is forbidden by the third Commandment?

A. The third Commandment forbids all unnecessary servile work and whatever else may hinder the due observance of the Lord's day,

359. Q. What are servile works?

A. Servile works are those which require labor rather of body than of mind.

360. Q. Are servile works on Sunday ever lawful?

A. Servile works are lawful on Sunday when the honor of God, the good of our neighbor, or necessity requires them.

LESSON THIRTY-THIRD

From the Fourth to the Seventh Commandment

Con-tempt′ (kŏn-tĕmpt′), making little of.

Di-rec′tion (dĭ-rĕk′shŭn), advice, counsel.

Ha′tred (hā′trĕd), strong dislike.

Mag′is-trates (măj′ĭs-trāts), public officials.

Re-venge′ (rē-vĕnj′), desire to pay back an injury.

Stub′born-ness (stŭb′ẽrn-nĕss), wanting to have our own way.

Su-pe′ri-ors (sū-pē′rĭ-ẽrz), those placed over us.

361. Q. What is the fourth Commandment?

A. The fourth Commandment is: "Honor thy father and thy mother."

362. Q. What are we commanded by the fourth Commandment?

A. We are commanded by the fourth Commandment to honor, love, and obey our parents in all that is not sin.

363. Q. Are we bound to honor and obey others than our parents?

A. We are also bound to honor and obey our bishops, pastors, magistrates, teachers, and other lawful superiors.

364. Q. Have parents and superiors any duties towards those who are under their charge?

A. It is the duty of parents and superiors to take good care of all under their charge and give them proper direction and example.

365. Q. What is forbidden by the fourth Commandment?

A. The fourth Commandment forbids all disobedience, contempt, and stubbornness towards our parents or lawful superiors.

366. Q. What is the fifth Commandment?

A. The fifth Commandment is: "Thou shalt not kill."

367. Q. What are we commanded by the fifth Commandment?

A. We are commanded by the fifth Commandment to live in peace and union with our neighbor, to respect his rights, to seek his spiritual and bodily welfare, and to take proper care of our own life and health.

368. Q. What is forbidden by the fifth Commandment?

A. The fifth Commandment forbids all willful murder, fighting, anger, hatred, revenge and bad example.

369. Q. What is the sixth Commandment?

A. The sixth Commandment is: "Thou shalt not commit adultery."

370. Q. What are we commanded by the sixth Commandment?

A. We are commanded by the sixth Commandment to be pure in thought and modest in all our looks, words, and actions.

371. Q. What is forbidden by the sixth Commandment?

A. The sixth Commandment forbids all unchaste freedom with another's wife or husband; also all immodesty with ourselves or others in looks, dress, words, or actions.

372. Q. Does the sixth Commandment forbid the reading of bad and immodest books and newspapers?

A. The sixth Commandment does forbid the reading of bad and immodest books and newspapers.

LESSON THIRTY-FOURTH

From the Seventh to the End of the Tenth Commandment

Back´bit´ing (băk´bīt´ĭng), talking evil of one who is absent.

Ban´ish (băn´ĭsh), to chase away.

Dam´age (dăm´ȧj), harm done to any one.

Ill´got´ten (ĭl´gŏt´ĕn), gotten unjustly.

Prop´er-ty (prŏp´ẽr-tĭ), that which belongs to a person.

Rash Judg´ments (răsh jŭj´mĕnts), thinking or saying evil things about another of which we are not sure.

Rep´u-ta´tion (rĕp´ū-tā´shŭn), good name.

Se´ri-ous-ly (sē´rĭ-ŭs-lĭ), greatly.

Slan´ders (slăn´dẽrz), wicked lies about another.

Un-just´ (ŭn-jŭst´), that which is against the rights of another.

373. Q. What is the seventh Commandment?

A. The seventh Commandment is: "Thou shalt not steal."

374. Q. What are we commanded by the seventh Commandment?

A. By the seventh Commandment we are commanded to give to all men what belongs to them and to respect their property.

375. Q. What is forbidden by the seventh Commandment?

A. The seventh Commandment forbids all unjust taking or keeping what belongs to another.

376. Q. Are we bound to restore ill-gotten goods?

A. We are bound to restore ill-gotten goods, or the value of them, as far as we are able; otherwise we cannot be forgiven.

377. Q. Are we obliged to repair the damage we have unjustly caused?

A. We are bound to repair the damage we have unjustly caused.

378. Q. What is the eighth Commandment?

A. The eighth Commandment is: "Thou shalt not bear false witness against thy neighbor."

379. Q. What are we commanded by the eighth Commandment?

A. We are commanded by the eighth Commandment to speak the truth in all things and to be careful of the honor and reputation of every one.

380. Q. What is forbidden by the eighth Commandment?

A. The eighth Commandment forbids all rash judgments, backbiting, slanders, and lies.

381. Q. What must they do who have lied about their neighbor and seriously injured his character?

A. They who have lied about their neighbor and seriously injured his character must repair the injury done as far as they are able, otherwise they will not be forgiven.

382. Q. What is the ninth Commandment?

A. The ninth Commandment is: "Thou shalt not covet thy neighbor's wife."

383. Q. What are we commanded by the ninth Commandment?

A. We are commanded by the ninth Commandment to keep ourselves pure in thought and desire.

384. Q. What is forbidden by the ninth Commandment?

A. The ninth Commandment forbids unchaste thoughts, desires of another's wife or husband, and all other unlawful impure thoughts and desires.

385. Q. Are impure thoughts and desires always sins?

A. Impure thoughts and desires are always sins, unless they displease us and we try to banish them.

386. Q. What is the tenth Commandment?

A. The tenth Commandment is: "Thou shalt not covet thy neighbor's goods."

387. Q. What are we commanded by the tenth Commandment?

A. By the tenth Commandment we are commanded to be content with what we have, and to rejoice in our neighbor's welfare.

388. Q. What is forbidden by the tenth Commandment?

A. The tenth Commandment forbids all desires to take or keep wrongfully what belongs to another.

LESSON THIRTY-FIFTH

On the First and Second Commandments of the Church

Ab-stain′ (ăb-stān′), not to eat meat.

Ab′sti-nence (ăb′stĭ-nĕns), doing without meat.

Con-trib′ute (kŏn-trĭb′ūt), to pay our share.

Fast (fȧst), to eat only one full meal in the day.

Kin′dred (kĭn′drĕd), blood relationship.

Mor′ti-fy (môr′tĭ-fī), to deaden, keep down.

Sol′em-nize (sŏl′ĕm-nīz), to have the wedding blessing and great display.

Third degree, second cousins.

Wit′ness-es (wĭt′nĕs-ĕz), the two who stand up with the marrying couple.

389. Q. Which are the chief commandments of the Church?

A. The chief commandments of the Church are six:

1. To hear Mass on Sundays and Holy Days of Obligation.
2. To fast and abstain on the days appointed.
3. To confess at least once a year.
4. To receive the Holy Eucharist during the Easter time.
5. To contribute to the support of our pastors.
6. Not to marry persons who are not Catholics, or who are related to us within the third degree of kindred, nor privately without witnesses, nor to solemnize marriage at forbidden times.

390. Q. Is it a mortal sin not to hear Mass on a Sunday or a Holy Day of Obligation?

A. It is a mortal sin not to hear Mass on a Sunday or a Holy Day of Obligation, unless we are excused for a serious reason. They also commit a mortal sin who, having others under their charge, hinder them from hearing Mass, without a sufficient reason.

391. Q. Why were Holy Days instituted by the Church?

A. Holy Days were instituted by the Church to recall to our minds the great mysteries of religion and the virtues and rewards of the Saints.

392. Q. How should we keep the Holy Days of Obligation?

A. We should keep the Holy Days of Obligation as we should keep the Sunday.

393. Q. What do you mean by fast-days?

A. By fast-days I mean days on which we are allowed but one full meal.

394. Q. What do you mean by days of abstinence?

A. By days of abstinence I mean days on which we are forbidden to eat flesh-meat, but are allowed the usual number of meals.

395. Q. Why does the Church command us to fast and abstain?

A. The Church commands us to fast and abstain, in order that we may mortify our passions and satisfy for our sins.[1]

1. "On the non-Lenten Fridays outside of Lent, the U.S. bishops conference obtained the permission of the Holy See for Catholics in the U.S. to substitute a penitential, or even a charitable, practice of their own choosing. They must do some penitential/charitable practice on these Fridays. For most people the easiest practice to consistently fulfill will be the traditional one, to abstain from meat. . . . During Lent, abstinence from meat on Fridays is obligatory in the United States as elsewhere." (www.ewtn.com/faith/lent/fast.html). —*Publisher*, 2010

396. Q. Why does the Church command us to abstain from flesh-meat on Fridays?

A. The Church commands us to abstain from flesh-meat on Fridays, in honor of the day on which our Saviour died.

LESSON THIRTY-SIXTH

On the Third, Fourth, Fifth, and Sixth Commandments of the Church

Cer´e-mo-ny (sĕr´ĕ-mō-nĭ), rite.
Fre´quent-ly (frē´kwĕnt-lĭ), often.
Nup´tial (nŭp´shăl), marriage.
Pomp (pŏmp), show, display.
Pre´cept (prē´sĕpt), command.
Pri´vate-ly (prī´văt-lĭ), secretly.
Wed´ded (wĕd´ĕd), married.

397. Q. What is meant by the command of confessing at least once a year?

A. By the command of confessing at least once a year is meant that we are obliged, under pain of mortal sin, to go to Confession within the year.

398. Q. Should we confess only once a year?

A. We should confess frequently, if we wish to lead a good life.

399. Q. Should children go to Confession?

A. Children should go to Confession when they are old enough to commit sin, which is commonly about the age of seven years.

400. Q. What sin does he commit who neglects to receive Communion during the Easter time?

A. He who neglects to receive Communion during the Easter time commits a mortal sin.

401. Q. What is the Easter time?

A. The Easter time is, in this country, the time between the first Sunday of Lent and Trinity Sunday.

402. Q. Are we obliged to contribute to the support of our pastors?

A. We are obliged to contribute to the support of our pastors, and to bear our share in the expenses of the church and school.

403. Q. What is the meaning of the commandment not to marry within the third degree of kindred?

A. The meaning of the commandment not to marry within the third degree of kindred is that no one is allowed to marry another within the third degree of blood relationship.

404. Q. What is the meaning of the command not to marry privately?

A. The command not to marry privately means that none should marry without the blessing of God's priests or without witnesses.

405. Q. What is the meaning of the precept not to solemnize marriage at forbidden times?

A. The meaning of the precept not to solemnize marriage at forbidden times is that during Lent and Advent the marriage ceremony should not be performed with pomp or a nuptial Mass.

406. Q. What is the nuptial Mass?

A. A nuptial Mass is a Mass appointed by the Church to invoke a special blessing upon the married couple.

407. Q. Should Catholics be married at a nuptial Mass?

A. Catholics should be married at a nuptial Mass, because they thereby show greater reverence for the holy Sacrament and bring richer blessings upon their wedded life.

LESSON THIRTY-SEVENTH

On the Last Judgment and the Resurrection, Hell, Purgatory, and Heaven

Con-demned′ (kŏn-dĕmd′), sentenced.
Deeds (dēdz), what one has done, good or bad.
De-prived′ (dē-prīvd′), kept from.
Dread′ful (drĕd′fŭl), terrible, awful.
Im-mor′tal (ĭm-môr′tăl), cannot die.
Per-mits′ (pĕr-mĭts′), does not hinder.
Pros′per (prŏs′pĕr), to get on well in this world.
Prov′i-dence (prŏv′ĭ-dĕns), God's way of dealing with us.
Ren′der (rĕn′dĕr), pay, give.
Tor′ments (tôr′mĕnts), pains.
Un′der-go′ (ŭn′dĕr-gō′) to stand or bear.
U-nit′ed (ū-nīt′ĕd), joined.

408. Q. When will Christ judge us?
A. Christ will judge us immediately after our death, and on the last day.

409. Q. What is the judgment called which we have to undergo immediately after death?
A. The judgment we have to undergo immediately after death is called the Particular Judgment.

410. Q. What is the judgment called which all men have to undergo on the last day?
A. The judgment which all men have to undergo on the last day is called the General Judgment.

411. Q. Why does Christ judge men immediately after death?

A. Christ judges men immediately after death to reward or punish them according to their deeds.

412. Q. What are the rewards or punishments appointed for men's souls after the Particular Judgment?

A. The rewards or punishments appointed for men's souls after the Particular Judgment are Heaven, Purgatory, and Hell.

413. Q. What is Hell?

A. Hell is a state to which the wicked are condemned, and in which they are deprived of the sight of God for all eternity, and are in dreadful torments.

414. Q. What is Purgatory?

A. Purgatory is a state in which those suffer for a time who die guilty of venial sins, or without having satisfied for the punishment due to their sins.

415. Q. Can the faithful on earth help the souls in Purgatory?

A. The faithful on earth can help the souls in Purgatory by their prayers, fasts, alms-deeds; by indulgences, and by having Masses said for them.

416. Q. If everyone is judged immediately after death, what need is there of a General Judgment?

A. There is need of a General Judgment, though everyone is judged immediately after death, that the providence of God, which, on earth, often permits the good to suffer and the wicked to prosper, may in the end appear just before all men.

417. Q. Will our bodies share in the reward or punishment of our souls?

A. Our bodies will share in the reward or punishment of our souls, because through the resurrection they will again be united to them.

418. Q. In what state will the bodies of the just rise?

A. The bodies of the just will rise glorious and immortal.

419. Q. Will the bodies of the damned also rise?

A. The bodies of the damned will also rise, but they will be condemned to eternal punishment.

420. Q. What is Heaven?

A. Heaven is the state of everlasting life in which we see God face to face, are made like unto Him in glory, and enjoy eternal happiness.

421. Q. What words should we bear always in mind?

A. We should bear always in mind these words of Our Lord and Saviour Jesus Christ: "What doth it profit a man if he gain the whole world and suffer the loss of his own soul, or what exchange shall a man give for his soul? For the Son of man shall come in the glory of His Father with His angels; and then will He render to every man according to his works."

MORNING PRAYERS

As soon as you awake, think of God. Make the Sign of the Cross and say:

✠ In the name of the Father, and of the Son, and of the Holy Ghost. Amen.

Then dress quickly and kneel down. Now say the *Our Father*, the *Hail Mary*, the *Apostles' Creed*, the *Confiteor* and the *Acts of Faith*, *Hope*, *Love* and *Contrition* which you have probably memorized. If you do not know them by heart you will find them on pages 1-5.

Then if you have time also say the following prayers:

To the Blessed Virgin

My Lady, and my Mother, remember I am thine; protect and defend me as thy property and possession.

To St. Joseph

Saint Joseph, model and patron of those who love the Sacred Heart of Jesus, pray for us.

To the Guardian Angel

Angel of God, my guardian dear,
To whom His love commits me here,
Ever this day be at my side,
To light and guard, to rule and guide. Amen.

God bless Papa and Mamma. God bless brothers and sisters, and all my friends. God bless me, and make me a good child.

For the Faithful Departed

Eternal rest give unto them, O Lord. And let perpetual light shine upon them. May they rest in peace. Amen.

Glory be to the Father, and to the Son, and to the Holy Ghost. As it was in the beginning, is now, and ever shall be, world without end. Amen.

Make the Sign of the Cross.

EVENING PRAYERS

Never go to bed without thanking God for all the benefits you have received during the day and during your whole life. Kneel down. Make the Sign of the Cross. Then say the *Our Father*, *Hail Mary*, the *Apostles' Creed*, the *Confiteor*, and *Glory Be*.

Now think how you have acted during the day. Are there any big sins on your soul? Any little sins? Try to tell Jesus how sorry you are for all your sins, and say the *Act of Contrition* (p. 4).

Jesus, Mary, Joseph, I give you my heart and my soul.
Jesus, Mary, Joseph, assist me in my last agony.
Jesus, Mary, Joseph, may I breathe forth my soul in peace with you.
O my God, bless my father, mother, and all my relatives and friends.
May the souls of the faithful departed, through the mercy of God, rest in peace. Amen.

Bless yourself with holy water.

✠ In the name of the Father, and of the Son, and of the Holy Ghost. Amen.

PRAYERS FOR MASS[1]

Remember that the church is the house of God, where the living God dwells. And where God is, His holy angels too are present. In church, therefore, be reverent and modest in your behavior, and always be on time. When you enter, bless yourself with holy water and go quietly to your seat, genuflect on your right knee and enter the pew.

Prayer before Mass

> O my God, I am only a child; help me to be attentive, and to pray with all my heart during this holy Mass.

The priest comes out to begin Mass.

Stand.

1. The Mass prayers are an arrangement of those contained in Father Finn's *Prayer Book for Catholic Youth* (also known as Father Finn's *Boys' and Girls' Prayer Book*). They follow closely in simplified language the spirit and liturgy of the "Ordinary of the Mass," so that children will become readily accustomed to using the Church's own prayers and follow the priest at the altar. The rubrics when to sit, stand, or kneel at Low Mass are given.

If it is found desirable to have the children recite prayers aloud and in unison at Mass, certain parts suitable for this purpose are marked with an asterisk (*).

The priest carries in his hands the chalice, covered with a cloth. The priest goes up to the middle of the altar, and sets down the chalice. Then he goes to the right side and opens the book.

After that he comes down to the foot of the altar, and makes the Sign of the Cross.

The Mass of the Catechumens

(From the Beginning to the Offertory)

Kneel.

*In the name of the Father, and of the Son, and of the Holy Ghost. Amen.

*I will go in to the altar of God, to God Who gives joy to my youth.

*Judge me, O God. Keep me safe from all evil.

Glory be to the Father, and to the Son and to the Holy Ghost.

As it was in the beginning, is now and ever shall be, world without end. Amen.

I will go in to the altar of God,
To God Who gives joy to my youth.

Here the priest makes the Sign of the Cross.

Our help is in the name of the Lord.
Who made Heaven and earth.

The priest, bowing down, says the *Confiteor*. Then the altar-boys bow and say it after him. Read it as on p. 2.

The priest goes up to the altar and says:

O Lord, we beg You, by the goodness of Your Saints whose relics are here, and of all Your Saints, to forgive us all our sins.

The Introit and Kyrie Eleison

The priest goes to the right side of the altar and reads from the book. Then going back to the middle of the altar he says the *Kyrie Eleison*.

The Gloria

Glory be to God on high, and on earth peace to men of good will. We praise You. We bless You. We glorify You. We give You thanks for Your great glory, O Lord God, heavenly King, God the Father almighty. O Lord God, Son of the Father, Who take away the sins of the world, have mercy on us. You only, O Jesus Christ, with the Holy Ghost, are most high in the Glory of God the Father. Amen.

The priest turns to the people and says:

The Lord be with you.
And with your spirit.

The Collect

The priest goes to the right side of the altar and reads from the book.

> *Let us pray: *Let Your grace and pity guide our hearts, we beg You, O Lord. For without You we cannot please You. Through Our Lord, Jesus Christ, Your Son, Who lives and reigns with You in the unity of the Holy Ghost, world without end. Amen.

The Epistle

The Epistle is a letter. Most of these letters were written by St. Paul. The priest now reads one of these. You may read the following:

> Dear children: Be happy, be good, be brave; agree with one another, and be at peace. The grace of Our Lord Jesus Christ, God's love, and the wisdom of the Holy Ghost be with you all. Amen.
>
> Thanks be to God.

The altar-boy carries the book to the left side of the altar. The priest bows at the middle of the altar and says a prayer.

The Gospel

The priest goes to the left and reads from the book.

Stand.

While Jesus was speaking to the people, mothers brought their children to Him, that He might bless them. The disciples told them not to bother Jesus. But Jesus said, "Suffer the little children to come to Me and forbid them not. For of such is the kingdom of Heaven." And Jesus blessed the children.

Praise be to You, O Christ.

Sit.

The priest now turns back to the middle of the altar and says the *Creed*. You also say it (see p. 1).

The Mass of the Faithful

(From the Offertory to the Communion)

The Offering of the Host

The priest takes the cloth off the chalice. Then he holds up a small gold plate on which is the bread, called the *host*.

*Take, O holy Father, almighty and eternal God, this spotless host which I, Your unworthy servant, offer to You for my many sins and for all who serve You, living and dead. May it help them and me to gain eternal life.

The priest goes to the right side of the altar. He pours wine and water into the chalice. Then the priest goes back to the middle of the altar and raises the chalice.

The Offering of the Chalice

*We offer You, O Lord, this chalice. May it help us and all the world to gain eternal life. Amen.

The priest goes to the right side of the altar to wash his hands.

Returning to the middle of the altar, the priest bows down and says some prayers. Then he turns to the people and says the *Orate Fratres*.

Now the priest prays in a low voice and then in a louder voice he says the Preface:

> Truly, it is right and just that we should at all times and in all places give thanks to You, O holy Lord, Father almighty, Who, with Your only Son and the Holy Ghost are one God, one Lord. All the angels daily praise You, singing with one voice:

**The Sanctus*

Holy, holy, holy Lord, God of hosts.
Heaven and earth are full of Your glory.
Hosanna in the highest.

The bell is rung three times.

Kneel.

The Canon[2]

The priest bows low and kisses the altar.

> O most merciful Father, we pray You, through Jesus Christ, Your Son, Our Lord, to take and bless these gifts. We offer them to You for Your holy Catholic Church, for our Pope and Bishop and for all those in the Catholic Faith.

Prayer for the Living

Be mindful, O Lord, of Your servants (*name those for whom you wish to pray especially*), and all who are now hearing this Mass. Hear, O Lord, the prayers they are offering for themselves, their friends and their families.

The Consecration of the Host

The priest now bends low over the host and says:

THIS IS MY BODY.

At these words, the bread is changed into the Body of Our Lord. The bell rings. The priest kneels and then raises the Sacred Body of Our Lord. Now look at the Sacred Host and say: "My Lord and my God." Then bow your head as the priest kneels again.

The Consecration of the Wine

The priest bends over the chalice and says:

THIS IS THE CHALICE OF MY BLOOD.

At these words, the wine becomes the Precious Blood of Our Lord. The bell rings. The priest kneels and then raises the Chalice. Now the priest continues to pray silently. Look at the Chalice and say: "Jesus in the Blessed Sacrament, have mercy on us."

The priest kneels. The bell rings again. The priest prays silently.

2. By a Decree of the Church (August 4, 1922), the prayers during the Canon, i.e., from the *Sanctus* to the *Pater Noster*, must be said in silence.

Prayer for the Dead

Remember also, O Lord, Your servants (*here name dead relatives and friends*) who have gone before us with the sign of faith and sleep the sleep of peace.

Now the priest says the *Pater Noster*. Say the *Our Father*. Soon after the priest strikes his breast and says the *Agnus Dei*.

The Priest's Communion

The priest after saying some prayers silently, takes the Sacred Host and paten in his left hand and striking his breast with the right hand says (the bell rings three times):

*O Lord, I am not worthy that You should enter under my roof. Say but the word and my soul shall be healed.

The priest bows down and receives the Body of Our Lord. He remains in prayer for a short time. Then he uncovers the Chalice and drinks the Sacred Blood of Our Lord.

The Communion of the People

The priest now opens the tabernacle and takes out the Blessed Sacrament to give Holy Communion to the people. Turning to the people and holding the ciborium in his left hand, he lifts up a Sacred Host to the people in his right hand. Now say with the priest three times:

"Lord, I am not worthy that You should enter my soul; say but the word and my soul shall be healed."

After the Communion

Having replaced the Blessed Sacrament in the tabernacle, the priest after taking water and wine, covers the Chalice and goes to the right side of the altar to read from the book. Then going back to the middle he turns to the people and says:

The Lord be with you.
And with your spirit.

Then the priest again goes to the right side of the altar and reads:

The Prayers after Communion

*Let us pray: We have been filled with Your gifts, O Lord. Grant that they may make us clean and strong. May the gift of this divine Sacrament keep us pure, O Lord. Through the help of the Blessed Virgin, of St. Joseph, of Sts. Peter and Paul and all the Saints, may it free us from all evil.

The priest goes back to the middle of the altar and turning to the people says:

The Lord be with you.
And with your spirit.
Go, the Mass is ended.
Thanks be to God.

The Blessing

The priest bows down and says a prayer. Then turning to the people he blesses them saying:

> May almighty God, the Father, Son, and Holy Ghost, bless you. Amen.

The priest goes to the left side of the altar.

Stand.

> The Lord be with you.
> And with your spirit.

The Last Gospel

The priest makes a cross on forehead, lips, and breast, and says the Gospel of St. John.

Remain standing until the priest has left the sanctuary or kneels down to say the prayers after Mass.

THE RIGHT MANNER OF CONFESSING[1]

Prayer before Examining Your Conscience

O Holy Spirit, help me to know all my sins. Help me to remember that Jesus died for me. Help me to make a good Confession and I promise that I will try never to sin again.

Now think of your sins.

Prayer before Entering the Confessional

O God, I am very sorry for all my sins. I promise that I will try to be good and never again to hurt You by sin. Dear Jesus, help me. Mother of God, pray that I may please Your Son by true sorrow for my sins.

1. From Father Finn's *Prayer Book for Catholic Youth.*

When your turn comes, go into the confession box. Make the Sign of the Cross and wait till the priest opens the little door. Say what you have been taught to say. Or you may say this:

> Bless me, Father, for I have sinned. It is (*say how long*) since my last Confession. Since then I have committed these sins.

Now tell all your sins and how many times you committed each. If there is something you don't know how to tell, just say, "Please help me, Father," and the priest will help you. After you have told all your sins, say what you have been taught to say. Or you may say:

> That is all, Father.

In case you have no big sins to confess, it is well to end your Confession with: "In my past life I sinned through anger or impurity" (or some sin that you know you did and that you are sorry for). The priest tells you what prayers to say for a penance. Then he tells you to say the *Act of Contrition*. When you come out, kneel down near the altar. Say your penance at once. Then thank God for being so good to you.

COMMUNION PRAYERS

Acts before Communion

Act of Faith

Jesus Christ, my Sovereign Lord, I firmly believe that Thou art really present in the Holy Eucharist, and that it is Thy body, Thy blood, Thy soul, and Thy divinity that I shall receive in that Adorable Sacrament.

Act of Hope

Thou hast said, O my God, that those hoping in Thee shall never be confounded. I place all my confidence in Thy promises, and I hope that, having nourished myself with Thy body on earth, I shall have the happiness of seeing and possessing Thee eternally in Heaven.

Act of Love

O my divine Jesus, Who hast so loved me as to nourish me with Thy adorable flesh, I love Thee with all my heart and above all things; I wish to live and die in Thy holy love.

Act of Humility

My Saviour and my God, Thou art all sanctity. I am not worthy that Thou shouldst enter my heart; yet, speak but the word and my soul shall be healed.

Act of Desire

My soul desires Thee, O my God! Thou art its joy and happiness. Come, O divine Jesus, come into my heart; it desires ardently to receive Thee.

Acts after Communion

Act of Adoration

I adore Thee, O Jesus, as the Lamb of God immolated for the salvation of mankind. I join in the profound adoration which the angels and Saints pay to Thee in Heaven.

Act of Thanksgiving

Lord, Thou hast looked on my unworthiness. I was sick, and Thou hast healed me. I was poor, and Thou hast bestowed upon me Thy numberless benefits. How shall I be able to thank Thee, O my Lord, for all Thy favors? I will invoke Thy holy Name, and eternally sing Thy mercies.

Act of Offering

What can I offer Thee, O my God, for the grace of having given Thyself to me? I consecrate to Thy glory my body, my soul, and all that I possess! Dispose of me according to Thy holy Will.

Act of Petition

My divine Redeemer, Thou hast taken possession of me. Do not let the enemy of my salvation ravish the precious treasure I bear in my heart. Preserve me from all sin, and defend me against temptation, that I may persevere until death in the practice of Thy holy law. Amen.

THE ROSARY OF THE BLESSED VIRGIN

The Five Joyful Mysteries

(Assigned for Mondays and Thursdays throughout the year, the Sundays of Advent and after Epiphany until Lent.)

First Mystery. The Annunciation.
Second Mystery. The Visitation.
Third Mystery. The Nativity.
Fourth Mystery. The Presentation.
Fifth Mystery. The Finding of the Child Jesus in the Temple.

The Five Sorrowful Mysteries

(For Tuesdays and Fridays throughout the year and Sundays in Lent.)

First Mystery. The Prayer and Bloody Sweat of our blessed Saviour in the Garden.
Second Mystery. The Scourging of Jesus at the Pillar.
Third Mystery. The Crowning of Jesus with Thorns.
Fourth Mystery. Jesus Carrying His Cross.
Fifth Mystery. The Crucifixion.

The Five Glorious Mysteries

(For Wednesdays and Saturdays throughout the year and Sundays after Easter until after Advent.)

First Mystery. The Resurrection.
Second Mystery. The Ascension.
Third Mystery. The Descent of the Holy Ghost.
Fourth Mystery. The Assumption.
Fifth Mystery. The Crowning of the Blessed Virgin.

THE STATIONS OF THE CROSS

A plenary indulgence can be gained each time one makes the Stations, subject to the usual conditions.

To make the Stations and gain the indulgences, no special prayer is required. We have but to begin at the first Station and go around to the last, thinking devoutly of the Passion and death of Christ

HYMNS

Come, Holy Ghost, Creator Blest

1. Come, Holy Ghost, Creator blest,
And in our hearts take up Thy rest;
Come with Thy grace and heavenly aid
To fill the hearts which Thou hast made.

2. O Comforter, to Thee we cry,
Thou heavenly Gift of God most
high,
Thou Fount of life and Fire of love,
And sweet Anointing from above.

3. Praise we the Father and the Son,
And Holy Spirit with them One;
And may the Son on us bestow
The gifts that from the Spirit flow.

O Salutaris

1. O Salutaris Hostia!
   Quae coeli pandis ostium:
   Bella premunt hostilia,
   Da robur, fer auxilium.

2. Uni trinoque Domino
   Sit sempiterna gloria,
   Qui vitam sine termino
   Nobis donet in Patria.
   Amen.

Tantum Ergo

1. Tantum ergo Sacramentum
   Veneremur cernui;
   Et antiquum documentum
   Novo cedat ritui;
   Praestet fides supplementum
   Sensuum defectui.

2. Genitori, Genitoque
   Laus et jubilatio,
   Salus, honor, virtus quoque
   Sit et benedictio;
   Procedenti ab utroque
   Compar sit laudatio.
   Amen.

V. Panem de coelo praestitisti eis.
R. Omne delectamentum in se habentem.

Adeste Fideles

1. Adeste, fideles,
Laeti triumphantes;
Venite, venite in Bethlehem;
Natum videte
Regem Angelorum,
Venite, adoremus,
Venite, adoremus,
Venite, adoremus Dominum.

2. Deum de Deo,
Lumen de lumine,
Gestant puellae viscera;
Deum verum,
Genitum non factum,
Venite, etc.

3. Cantet nunc Io!
Chorus Angelorum;
Cantet nunc aula coelestium.
Gloria
In excelsis Deo,
Venite, etc.

4. Ergo, qui natus
Die hodierna,
Jesu! tibi sit gloria,
Patris aeterni
Verbum caro factum,
Venite, etc.

Jesus, My Lord, My God

(Rev. F. W. Faber)

1. Jesus, my Lord, my God, my all!
   How can I love Thee as I ought?
And how revere this wondrous gift,
   So far surpassing hope or thought?

Chorus Sweet Sacrament! We Thee adore,
Oh, make us love Thee more and more,
Oh, make us love Thee more and more.

2. Had I but Mary's sinless heart
   To love Thee with, my dearest King,
Oh, with what bursts of fervent praise
   Thy goodness, Jesus, would I sing!

To Jesus' Heart All Burning

(Rev. A. J. Christie, S.J.)

1. To Jesus' Heart, all burning
   With fervent love for men,
My heart with fondest yearning
   Shall raise the joyful strain.

Chorus While ages course along,
Blest be with loudest song
The Sacred Heart of Jesus
By every heart and tongue.

2. O Heart for me on fire
   With love no man can speak,
   My yet untold desire
   God gives me for Thy sake.

3. Too true I have forsaken
   Thy flock by wilful sin;
   Yet now let me be taken
   Back to Thy fold again.

Jesus, Gentlest Saviour

(Rev. F. W. Faber)

1. Jesus, gentlest Saviour!
   God of might and power;
   Thou Thyself art dwelling
   In us at this hour.
   Nature cannot hold Thee,
   Heav'n is all too strait
   For Thine endless glory,
   And Thy royal state.

2. Out beyond the shining
   Of the farthest star,
   Thou art ever stretching
   Infinitely far.
   Yet the hearts of children
   Hold what worlds cannot,
   And the God of wonders
   Loves the lowly spot.

Jesus! Saviour of My Soul

1. Jesus! Saviour of my soul,
   Let me to Thy refuge fly,
   While the nearer waters roll,
   While the tempest still is nigh.

Chorus
Hide me, O my Saviour, hide
   Till the storm of life is past;
Safe into Thy haven guide,
   O receive my soul at last.
Jesus! Saviour of my soul,
   Let me to Thy refuge fly;
Ave, Ave, Jesus mild,
   Deign to hear Thy lowly child.

2. Other refuge have I none,
   Hangs my helpless soul on Thee,
   Leave, oh, leave me not alone,
   Still support and strengthen me.

Jesus, the Very Thought of Thee

(Rev. E. Caswall)

1. Jesus, the very thought of Thee
   With rapture fills my breast;
   But sweeter far Thy Face to see,
   And in Thy presence rest.

2. Nor voice can sing, nor heart can frame,
   Nor can the mem'ry find
   A sweeter sound than Thy blest Name,
   O Saviour of mankind!

3. Jesus, our only joy be Thou,
   As Thou our prize wilt be;
   O Jesus, be our glory now
   And through eternity.

What Happiness Can Equal Mine?

(Rev. F. W. Faber)

1. What happiness can equal mine?
   I've found the object of my love:
   My Jesus dear, my King Divine,
   Is come to me from heav'n above;
   He chose my heart for His abode,
   He there becomes my daily bread;
   There on me flows His healing blood;
   There with His flesh my soul is fed.

Chorus What happiness can equal mine?
I've found the object of my love:
My Jesus dear, my King Divine,
Is come to me from heav'n above.

2. I am my love's, and He is mine:
In me He dwells, in Him I live;
What greater treasures could I find?
And could, ye heavens, a greater give?
O sacred banquet, heav'nly feast!
O overflowing source of grace,
Where God the food, and man, the guest,
Meet and unite in sweet embrace!

The Love of Jesus

1. O the priceless love of Jesus:
O the strength of grace divine;
All His gifts are showered upon me,
All His blessings may be mine.
He is throned in Heavenly glory
Where no sin nor death can be;
Yet He loves me in this darkness,
Yet He does not turn from me.

2. I am blind, and poor, and wretched,
   By temptations sorely tried;
 Yet His watchful care abounding
   Keeps me ever at His side.
 He is God and King Eternal,
   Higher than all height can be;
 Yet His Heart is with me always,
   Yet He stoopeth down to me.

Holy God, We Praise Thy Name

(Rev. C. Walworth)

1. Holy God, we praise Thy name,
   Lord of all, we bow before Thee!
 All on earth Thy sceptre claim,
   All in heav'n above adore Thee.
 Infinite Thy vast domain,
   Everlasting is Thy name.

2. Hark! the loud celestial hymn,
   Angel choirs above are raising!
 Cherubim and Seraphim,
   In unceasing chorus praising.
 Fill the heavens with sweet accord;
   Holy! Holy! Holy Lord.

Hail, Heavenly Queen!

1. Hail, heavenly Queen! Hail, foamy ocean star!
   O be our guide, diffuse thy beams afar;
   Hail, Mother of God! above all virgins blest,
   Hail, happy gate of heav'n's eternal rest.

Chorus Hail foamy ocean star! Hail, heav'nly Queen!
   O be our guide to endless joys unseen.

2. "Hail, full of grace," with Gabriel we repeat;
   Thee, Queen of heav'n, from him we learn to greet;
   Then give us peace which heav'n alone can give,
   And dead thro' Eve, thro' Mary let us live.

Mother Dear, Oh, Pray for Me

1. Mother dear, oh, pray for me,
   Whilst far from heav'n and thee
   I wander in a fragile bark,
   O'er life's tempestuous sea;
   O Virgin Mother, from thy throne,
   So bright in bliss above,
   Protect thy child and cheer my path,
   With thy sweet smile of love.

Chorus Mother dear, remember me,
   And never cease thy care,
   Till in Heaven eternally
   Thy love and bliss I share.

2. Mother dear, oh, pray for me,
   Should pleasure's siren lay
 E'er tempt thy child to wander far
   From virtue's path away;
 When thorns beset life's devious way,
   And darkling waters flow,
 Then, Mary, aid thy weeping child,
   Thyself a mother show.

Ora Pro Me

1. Ave Maria! bright and pure,
   Hear, O hear me when I pray,
 Pains and pleasures try the pilgrim
   On his long and dreary way.
 Fears and perils are around me,
   Ave Maria! bright and pure,
     Ora pro me, ora pro me.

2. Ave Maria! Queen of Heaven,
   Teach, O teach me to obey,
 Lead me on, tho' fierce temptations
   Stand and meet me in the way.
 When I fail and faint, my Mother,
   Ave Maria! bright and pure,
     Ora pro me, ora pro me.

I'll Sing a Hymn to Mary

(Rev. Fr. Wyse)

I'll sing a hymn to Mary,
The Mother of my God,
The Virgin of all Virgins,
Of David's royal blood.
Oh, teach me, holy Mary
A loving song to frame,
When wicked men blaspheme thee
To love and bless thy name.

When troubles dark afflict me
In sorrow and in care,
Thy light doth ever guide me
O beauteous Morning Star.
Lo, I'll be ever ready
Thy goodly help to claim,
When wicked men blaspheme thee
I'll love and bless thy name.

Daily, Daily Sing to Mary

1. Daily, daily sing to Mary
Sing, my soul, her praises due;
All her feasts, her actions worship,
With the heart's devotion true.
Lost in wond'ring contemplation,
Be her majesty confess'd;
Call her Mother, call her Virgin,
Happy Mother, Virgin blest.

2. She is mighty to deliver;

Call her, trust her lovingly;
When the tempest rages round thee,
She will calm the troubled sea.
Gifts of Heaven she has given,
Noble Lady, to our race;
She the Queen who decks her subject,
With the light of God's own grace.

Hymn to St. Joseph

1. With grateful hearts we breathe today
The tender accents of our love.
We carol forth a little lay
To thee, great Saint in Heaven above.

Chorus O Joseph dear, from thy bright throne,
Incline thine ear unto our prayer.
And o'er us all as o'er thine own,
Extend thy fond paternal care,
And o'er us all as o'er thine own,
Extend thy fond paternal care,
Extend thy fond paternal care.

2. More favored than earth's greatest king.
Thou wert the guardian of that Child,
Around whose crib full choirs did sing,
With cadenced voices soft and mild.

Dear Guardian of Mary

(Rev. F. W. Faber)

1. Dear Guardian of Mary! dear nurse of her child!
Life's ways are full weary, the desert is wild;
Bleak sands are all round us, no home can we see;
Sweet Spouse of Our Lady! we lean upon thee.
2. For thou to the pilgrim art father and guide,
And Jesus and Mary felt safe at thy side;
Ah! blessed Saint Joseph, how safe should I be,
Sweet Spouse of Our Lady! if thou wert with me.

Dear Angel, Ever at My Side

(Rev. F. W. Faber)

1. Dear Angel, ever at my side,
    How loving must thou be,
To leave thy home in Heaven to guide
    A little child like me.

2. Thy beautiful and shining face
    I see not, though so near;
The sweetness of thy soft, low voice
    I am too deaf to hear.

Hymn at the Communion

O Lord, I am not worthy
   That Thou shouldst come to me,
But speak the words of comfort,
   My spirit healed shall be.

And humbly I'll receive Thee,
   The bridegroom of my soul,
No more by sin to grieve Thee,
   Or fly Thy sweet control.